MW00474507

The Boys
of
Riverside

The Boys
of
Riverside

A Deaf Football Team and a Quest for Glory

THOMAS FULLER

Doubleday

New York

Jacket image: Members of the California School for the Deaf,
Riverside Cubs football team by Luis Sinco / *Los Angeles Times* /
Getty Images; background by FanPro / Getty Images
Jacket design by Michael J. Windsor
Book design by Michael Collica

Library of Congress Cataloging-in-Publication Data
Names: Fuller, Thomas (Journalist), author.
Title: The boys of Riverside / Thomas Fuller.
Description: First edition. | New York : Doubleday, [2024].
Identifiers: LCCN 2023028148 (print) | LCCN 2023028149 (ebook) |
ISBN 9780385549875 (hardcover) | ISBN 9780385549882 (ebook)
Subjects: LCSH: Deaf athletes—California—Riverside. |
Deaf youth—California—Riverside. | High school athletes—
California—Riverside. | Football players—California—Riverside.
Classification: LCC GV584.5.R58 F85 2024 (print) |
LCC GV584.5.R58 (ebook) | DDC 796.3309794/97—dc23/eng/20240313
LC record available at https://lccn.loc.gov/2023028148
LC ebook record available at https://lccn.loc.gov/2023028149

MANUFACTURED IN THE UNITED STATES OF AMERICA

1 3 5 7 9 10 8 6 4 2

First Edition

To Jocelyn, Harrison, and Sophie,
for your love and patience as I rumbled off to Riverside

Contents

Prologue   1

1. Phillip   5

2. Hell Week   8

3. A School Among the Orange Groves   14

4. A Taste of Victory   19

5. Hearing with Your Eyes   24

6. On a Roll   31

7. Stamina   38

8. The Sound of the Sun   41

9. Frowned upon by the Gods   51

10. The FaceTime Revolution   61

11. Deafness as a Choice   64

12. Fame   73

13. The Deaf Brain   80

14. Avalon   86

15. Battered   93

16. A Football? But It's Not Round   96

17. Underdog Meets Top Dog   103

18. Finishing with a Bang   107

19. "No Hope Left"   113

20. Unfinished Business   117

21. "Full Sprints!"   120

22. "Be Hungry for It! Be Angry!"   125

23. "They Think We Are Nothing"   130

24. Deaf Versus Deaf   144

25. Playing a Deaf Legend   154

26. Felix   161

27. The Speech   169

28. "I'm Playing! I'm Playing!"   177

29. The Wicks and the Bombs   184

30. An Apparition on the Practice Field   192

31. Playing with Fire   200

32. The Psychology of Winning   210

33. The Throw   213

34. Blocking and Tackling   216

35. College Dreams   221

36. "That Kid Can Play Anywhere"   227

37. "You Guys Deserved This"   232

Acknowledgments   237

The Boys
of
Riverside

Prologue

Sometimes a journey begins with an email. This one was a routine message sent to journalists from the California Department of Education, a note applauding the undefeated season of a deaf high school football team in Riverside, east of Los Angeles. The deaf school was founded a few years after World War II, but in seven decades none of its sports teams had ever made it to a championship, let alone prevailed in one. Now the California School for the Deaf, Riverside was in the playoffs. The email concluded with a plea for assistance: please help the school upgrade their facilities and write a check with "bleachers" on the memo line.

My job for *The New York Times* was San Francisco bureau chief. That meant covering wildfires and homelessness, deaths of despair on the streets of California cities and mass shootings. These topics are in line with the arc of my three decades in journalism, most of which have been spent abroad for the *Times* writing about natural disasters and military coups, uprisings and financial crises. It was heavy stuff, both the stories and the reporting. I had interviewed a rogue general in Thailand who was killed by a sniper as I was asking him a question. The bullet had whizzed over my head. I had counted bodies floating down a river after a terrible cyclone in Myanmar.

Then along came this group of high school kids and their quest for a championship. Something about the Riverside Cubs pulled me in like metal to a magnet. Riverside was seven hours away from my home in the East Bay of San Francisco. I got into my car and barreled down the eight-lane California freeways, arriving just in time to meet with the players and to watch them crush their opponents in the second round of the playoffs. I interviewed the coach of the losing team, and he told me he had never competed against a squad that communicated so fluidly, and so well.

Reporting this story introduced me to the world of eight-man football, a division for smaller schools in California that have trouble fielding eleven-player teams. The California School for the Deaf, Riverside had just fifty-one boys in its regular high school academic programs. Nearly half of them were on the football team.

I came to appreciate the eight-man game. It was fast, hard-hitting, and a little more down in the dirt than eleven-man ball. Sometimes literally. At Trona High School, in a mining community in the Mojave Desert, the team plays their games on sand. The field is known as the Pit, part of the desolate landscape that envelops the town on the edge of Death Valley.

The eight-man division includes schools on the endless farms and ranchlands of the Central Valley, on Indian reservations, and perched high in mountain passes. There's even an eight-man team on Santa Catalina Island, an hour's ferry ride into the blue-green waters of the Pacific Ocean, where home-field advantage comes with the hope that the opposing team gets woozy on the boat ride over.

Smaller and far-flung does not mean less athletic. Big names have come out of California's eight-man football programs, including Josh Allen, the Buffalo Bills quarterback, who played for Firebaugh High School in a farming town in the Central Valley.

The 1994 Heisman Trophy winner, Rashaan Salaam, played on an eight-man team in San Diego.

In reporting the book, I came to see the Cubs as a flesh-and-blood realization of the American dream. Coaches and players had backgrounds that spanned the globe. Their parents were from Mexico, Romania, El Salvador, Ethiopia. The team's defensive coordinator, Kaveh Angoorani, was born in Iran to a mother who was deeply distraught when she discovered her son was deaf. She sent Kaveh (pronounced "kaa-vey") to the United States, where he thrived in the deaf community and took up this curious game with an oblong ball. Football would become a central part of Kaveh's new American identity, one that he embraced so enthusiastically that his idea of retirement was to buy a Harley-Davidson and ride into the California desert.

I marveled at the challenges that some of the players faced off the field. Phillip Castaneda, a lightning-fast running back, was homeless and slept in his father's car in a Target parking lot across from the school. His love of football motivated him to get up every morning, wash his face in the Target bathroom, and go to class.

The article I wrote about the Cubs for the *Times* got the school a lot of attention and put intense pressure on the team to win. I decided to put my career on hold, give up my position as San Francisco bureau chief, and follow the team for an entire season. It was a dream journey and a window into Deaf Culture, a term that many deaf people capitalize because it encompasses an entire class of people and their way of life. I was honored that the players, coaches, and administrators at the school trusted me—someone with little prior knowledge about deafness—to tell their story. I interviewed historians and linguists, psychologists and a neurosurgeon, all of whom had contributed to the incredible leaps in knowledge about the complex structure of sign language and how the human brain adapts itself to deafness by enhancing other senses.

The sports program at the California School for the Deaf had endured indignities for years. Visiting teams would sometimes talk about how it would be embarrassing to lose to a deaf team. During their many years with a losing record, the football team had the sinking feeling their opponents came expecting an easy win. Many of the talented athletes on the Cubs had previously played football in weekend leagues, with hearing people, and they had come away feeling lonely and alienated, unable to take part in huddles or team meetings. At Riverside, they came together as a squad with a sense of mission, an all-deaf team and coaching staff. They were underdogs, but they had something immeasurable. They had a brotherhood.

As I stood on the sidelines watching the team practice day after day, I witnessed a passion for the game of football. I was inspired by the players and their relentless pursuit of that championship ring. That email, which came as the pandemic was raging across a bitterly divided United States, led me to realize that this team's journey, a tale of belonging and excellence, was the story I wanted to write. It felt like a salve at a time of such turmoil in the country.

More than a hundred high schools in California play eight-man ball, and only two of them are deaf schools. The Cubs were determined to show the world that deafness was no impediment to sporting glory. On the contrary, they wanted to prove that being deaf on the gridiron gave them an edge.

1

Phillip

The story begins before the reporters and the television correspondents flocked to interview the team. Before the offers from movie producers, before the National Football League invited the captains to participate in the Super Bowl coin toss. Before success.

The story begins in the late summer of 2021, just as California, the nation, and the world were emerging from the worst of the coronavirus pandemic. It begins with a newcomer to the school, Phillip Castaneda, in the parking lot where he slept.

Phillip had a morning ritual. He would scamper out of his father's Nissan Sentra, get his clothes from a suitcase in the trunk of the car, and then slide back into the car to get dressed for the day. He had to wait until 8:00 a.m., when Target opened its doors, to slip into the entrance, hang a left, and head for the bathroom.

The backseat of his father's compact car was his bedroom. And if he looked out the car's windows, he could see, across four lanes of traffic, the football field where he hoped to shine. Football was his first love. He had played on various teams when he was younger, and despite his short stature and slight frame, he had impressed coaches with his speed and his toughness. Now he planned on displaying his talents across the street, on the varsity football team of the California School for the Deaf in Riverside, California.

Phillip's father, Jude Ward Castaneda, had driven to Riverside with the express purpose of giving his son a place to sleep. The Nissan was the only shelter he had the means to provide. Each night, Jude Castaneda would find a spot, preferably away from other vehicles, in the lot on Arlington Avenue. In addition to Target, there was a Yum Yum Donuts, where Phillip would also sometimes use the bathroom, a small Pizza Hut, a nail salon, a cannabis dispensary, and a dentist's office. It was a classic California strip mall. Phillip scraped together enough money to get a membership to the gym down the road, where he could use the showers. Every night, at around midnight, after all the shops had closed, Jude and his girlfriend would settle into the front seats of the car and Phillip would have the back to himself. All three are deaf, but Phillip had just enough hearing that he could make out the blaring horns of freight trains passing on tracks a few dozen yards away.

In his younger years, Phillip's father had been a gifted athlete and had competed as a wrestler in the International Games for the Deaf, the Deaf Olympics. But by his own assessment, Jude Castaneda had traveled down the wrong path, becoming hooked on methamphetamines and spending time in prison for domestic violence and violating probation. He had stayed out of trouble for the past decade, he said, and now he hoped that he could give his son a better chance at life. "I didn't want him to be messed up like me," he said in a conversation on the sidelines of a football game.

California has around 12 percent of the nation's total population, but almost a third of its homeless. Living in a car, in a tent, or on a piece of cardboard has become distressingly common in the Golden State, where the average house costs $700,000. For Phillip Castaneda, homelessness was compounding an already tough childhood. He had been enrolled in six different schools and had struggled in all of them. Studying English, a language with all its peculiar spellings and syntax, was especially tedious. You could say that learning English for Phillip was the equivalent of an American person with perfect hearing studying a foreign language, Portuguese or Swahili, take your pick, but never being allowed to hear it spoken. American Sign Language, which is as different from English as two languages can be, is his native tongue. But of course "native tongue" is a term, like so many in English, that is not quite adapted to the deaf world.

Born just outside San Francisco and raised in the Central Valley, the vast agricultural expanse that produces everything from almonds to truckloads of tomatoes that get mashed into a good share of the world's ketchup, Phillip was dealt a difficult hand from the start. His mother, also deaf, had been born in El Salvador and moved to California when she was a child. Among other ailments, she had a debilitating case of rheumatoid arthritis, the disease where the body's immune system attacks its own tissue. It left her unable to work and relying on government disability checks.

As a teenager, Phillip had played football with hearing kids in and around the Central Valley city of Modesto. A friend offered to pay the $400 in fees that the league required. Phillip excelled on the field, but it was difficult being the only deaf person on a hearing team. Not understanding the instructions for some of the drills at practice, Phillip made sure he was always at the back of the line, where he could watch his teammates go first. But he loved the sport and told his family he wanted to play in the National Football League.

"Football was his escape," his sister, Priscilla Castaneda, said. "Football gives him joy."

2

Hell Week

O n the first day of practice of the 2021 season, Galvin Drake
pulled into the parking lot of the California School for the
Deaf in Riverside, music blaring. The thumping beats of Daft Punk
and Damian Lazarus were so loud it seemed as if they could loosen
the bolts holding together his green 2005 Toyota Camry. Galvin
couldn't hear the melodies or the lyrics, but it didn't matter. Music
had a different meaning for him than it did for hearing people.
The beats pulsed through his seat. He didn't listen to music; he *felt*
it. Late at night when he would drive near his home in Riverside,
Galvin would turn it down, as a courtesy for his hearing neighbors.
But on campus, he let it rip, often with the windows open.

Galvin was the assistant varsity football coach at the school, or
CSDR, as everyone calls it. He was the team's enforcer, lecturing
the players on the importance of weight lifting and eating well. No
junk food and soda during football season, he told the student athletes. He looked the part. He could deadlift 405 pounds—not 400,
but 405, he noted—and had the bulging muscles to prove it. He
ended his text messages with a flexing biceps emoji. But on this first
day of practice he was worried. The pandemic had forced the cancellation of football the year before, and everyone had languished

in front of computer screens, attending their classes remotely on Zoom and playing video games when class was over. Many of the players were overweight. All were out of shape.

The pandemic set back millions of students across America, but for deaf children it was especially hard. Many lived in homes or neighborhoods where no one spoke their language. School was the place they found peers, they learned to advocate for themselves, they came out of their shells. "When COVID happened, all they had was this little tiny screen on Zoom," one administrator at the school said. "School was their access to the world."

Keith Adams, the burly head coach of the football program, with a shaved head perpetually tanned by the California sun, could relate to what the pandemic had done to his players' bodies. He had gained thirty pounds himself. On day one of practice, Adams arrived with cases of Gatorade that he had bought at Costco to ward off dehydration. He was determined to get his players into fighting shape.

.   .   .

August in Riverside can feel like the inside of a pizza oven. Unlike the California coast, which benefits from the natural air-conditioning blowing in from the Pacific Ocean, Riverside is one mountain range away from the Mojave Desert. To avoid the worst of the heat, the coaches had scheduled their first weeks of practices for the evening, when temperatures typically fell into the low nineties. The players had a name for the first days of conditioning: Hell Week.

Phillip Castaneda didn't have far to travel to get to practice. He walked across the street from the Target parking lot. He cast an eye at his new teammates. They were greeting one another like long-lost relatives. High school students get only four years to prove themselves on the football field. This cohort would get only three. The cancellation of the previous year's season had made the players hungry to play again, to be teammates again, to block and tackle. They had missed the physicality of the game that came so naturally to them. In the plainest of terms, they were restless boys who wanted to hit again.

The first day began with Coach Adams gathering the team for orientation meetings in the air-conditioned bliss of the athletic facility. This could have been a meeting of any football team in America, coaches and players sitting on plastic folding chairs in a colorless classroom discussing their hopes for the season. But there was an important difference for the Cubs, a kind of inescapable togetherness. Teenagers, boys in particular, are known for their adolescent grunt years, for eyes-cast-down, monosyllabic conversations. This was rarely the case in Cubs meetings. Communicating in sign language required unbroken eye contact; it demanded that a listener watch not only the hands but also the slightest nuances in facial expressions. When Keith Adams reminded his players, as he did so often, that the team would succeed only if everyone did their job, all eyes were on him. Most days, Adams did not need to ask for his players' attention: it was ingrained in Deaf Culture. The boys were, by necessity, locked in.

Much of what the team discussed on this first day was practical. Face masks were obligatory inside, Coach Adams told them. School was back in session, but the coronavirus still stalked students and teachers. Write your name on your water bottle and don't share it, he said. Only eight people allowed in the weight room at once.

The weight room, which had two heavy doors that automatically locked unless you found a way to prop them open, ran along a corridor that led to the locker rooms. When one stood in that hallway looking through the sealed-shut windows, it was nearly impossible to hear people inside the weight room. But this was no obstacle for the Cubs. They could effortlessly converse through the thick glass, one person signing in the hallway to another inside using the weights.

If it had been a hearing school, a student might be able to bang on the door loudly enough for someone to open it. That wasn't an option for the Cubs. No one would know you were knocking. The Cubs were window people, not door people. Window versus door; it was a leitmotif in deaf art and literature.

At the team's first gathering, Phillip could see the strong family element at the very core of the Cubs: the team's star quarterback, Trevin Adams, was the son of Coach Adams, and Trevin's younger brother, Kaden, was also on the team. It was a dynamic that gave Coach Adams all the more incentive to succeed. Keith Adams was both coach and father. As for Trevin, who had inherited his father's stockiness and drive, no one—not players on the team or their adversaries—would ever question why he was quarterback and not someone else. From his time playing in little leagues and in middle school, Trevin had always shown an outsized talent and passion for the game of football.

After the team finished its meeting, the players headed out to the school's rutted grass field ringed by a dirt track. Coach Adams and his assistants split them into four stations, where they would run various drills. They did calisthenics and footwork. Then Adams assembled the team at the goal line and told them to sprint back and forth across the field. In eight-man ball, the field is shortened to 80 yards, so they went to and fro, 160 yards at a time.

The players stood at the goal line for these, their first sprints of the season. Among them were Trevin; Jory Valencia, a stringy wide receiver whose brother, also deaf, would soon head off to Europe to play professional basketball; and Felix Gonzales, the most versatile player on the team, on the short side but very fast. All three had been teammates in middle school, and they, with a few other players, were the heart of the Cubs. They, like other players on the team, had also benefited from more stable childhoods than Phillip Castenada's. Their parents had a variety of mostly middle- and working-class jobs: teacher, mechanic, Amazon warehouse worker, carpenter, mail sorter at the post office, hotel housekeeper, substance abuse counselor. In the United States, more than 90 percent of deaf children are born to hearing parents, a stark communication barrier between mother, father, and child. Parents and their sons or daughters spoke different languages. But the majority of the players on the Cubs came from deaf families, giving them added stability at home: they could communicate effortlessly with their parents in American Sign Language.

Phillip was already out of breath from the previous set of drills, but he wanted to show his new teammates his speed. He was five feet, six inches and 130 pounds, a lightweight in boxing terms. But he was so fast that Felix Gonzales would later remark that when he ran, it looked as if he didn't have legs, like the roadrunner in the cartoon.

Phillip ran the sprints hard but then suddenly took a detour off to the side of the field. He fell to his knees and retched. He got up and then threw up again, so many times, in fact, that he felt like a human water fountain, kneeling and gurgling on the sidelines and worrying that the coaches and his new teammates were looking at him as a lost cause. But he was not the only one. Ten players, nearly half the team, vomited in practice, some of them dashing to the locker room to heave in the relative privacy of a bathroom stall. Cody Metzner, the team's veteran running back who had lifted weights at home during the pandemic, kept his lunch down. But he was panting for breath, feeling awful, and nearly passed out.

Coach Adams was alarmed. Players at other schools had been able to meet for conditioning during the pandemic. But CSDR was a boarding school as well as a day school. The students who lived in the Riverside area commuted every day to school and could have theoretically come to practice. But the boarders at the school came from across Southern California: San Luis Obispo near the coast, Bakersfield in the Central Valley, San Diego along the Mexican border. They had gone home during the distance learning phase of the pandemic. There had been no way to get the team together.

Coach Adams decided to cut short the two-hour practice after just half an hour. It was a small team, just twenty-one players, and he couldn't afford for anyone to quit. The coaches were also worried about pushing the players too hard in the heat. A year earlier, a fifteen-year-old football player in Riverside County had died from heatstroke after an intense round of sprints.

This was an inauspicious start for the season, Keith Adams thought to himself. For the entire pandemic lockdown he had been awaiting the day when he could energize this football program. They had suffered losing seasons—more losses than wins—for the past eight years. In fact, since the CSDR football program began in the 1950s, the Cubs had been tormented by loss. The archives showed the football team had managed just nine winning seasons, and a handful of years where they won and lost an equal number of games. But they had fifty-one losing seasons. And in nearly a dozen of those, they had not managed to win a single game.

3

A School Among the
Orange Groves

Until the 1950s, there was only one state-run school exclusively dedicated to educating deaf students in California, an institution in San Francisco initially called the Society for the Instruction and Maintenance of the Indigent Deaf and Dumb and the Blind. The school, founded in the wake of the gold rush of the mid-nineteenth century, later became known by its shortened name, the California School for the Deaf, and moved across the bay to Berkeley. It became a center of Deaf Culture in California and spawned a tight-knit alumni network. But in a state that runs eight hundred miles north to south, getting to Berkeley was a long journey for families living closer to the Mexican border than the San Francisco Bay. As Southern California boomed after World War II, and Los Angeles took its place as the state's preeminent city, a movement to establish a deaf school in the Southlands, as the bottom half of the state was called, took root.

Advocates for the new school were successful, and in 1946, with the passage of a bill in the state legislature and the signature of Governor Earl Warren, the state, after months of searching, committed itself to establishing a school for the deaf in Riverside. At the time, Riverside was a small city of fifty thousand people best known for its acres and acres of orange groves.

Had it not been for a canal that early settlers built, much of Riverside would have remained a dusty landscape of cacti. But water had changed everything, and the desert bloomed with citrus. Riverside was forever changed by the cultivation of a sweet and seedless orange sent by American missionaries in Brazil in the 1870s. Initially known as the Riverside navel, it gave rise to an industry. Refrigerated train cars dispatched the fruit to the northern reaches of the United States, where oranges were still considered a luxury.

To the outside world, Orange County, by virtue of its name, has often been thought of as the center of the citrus business in California. But it was Riverside where it all began and flourished. A marketing cooperative created in the city spearheaded the promotion of oranges. It would come to be known as Sunkist, one of the most recognized brands in the country and beyond. By the late nineteenth century, Riverside was among the wealthiest towns in California, attracting dignitaries and investors to its orchards. In 1885, Riverside oranges won gold medals at the New Orleans World's Fair.

Not far from where the CSDR campus sits today, President Theodore Roosevelt visited the city in 1903 and took part in a ceremony to replant one of the original navel orange trees that the missionaries had dispatched from South America. A picture of Roosevelt at the ceremony in downtown Riverside shows the president wearing a top hat and holding a shovel next to a mound of dirt and a crowd of onlookers. The budding empire of the navel orange brought to Riverside a Mediterranean cachet. The Sunkist brand was a marketing juggernaut not only selling oranges but also sending a message to the rest of the country: California was a dreamscape of endless sunshine.

In 1948, the site chosen for the southern branch of the California School for the Deaf was a field of barley and orange trees. According to an account in the four-hundred-page, meticulously documented book *The CSDR Story,* by an alumnus, Kevin Struxness, deaf advocates liked the site for a number of reasons, including the fact that it was not near any mental hospitals or homes for juvenile delinquents. Too often in other states, deaf schools were grouped together with those institutions and "carried the stigma of the asylum or charitable institution," as Struxness put it.

The site of the future school, seventy-four acres framed by dirt roads, was purchased for $68,500, or $925 an acre, a pittance by modern California standards. Half a century later, the land would be valued at more than a hundred times that.

Those who had advocated for the creation of the school received a telegram from Sacramento in January 1949: "The finest school for the deaf in the United States will be built this year at Riverside."

The telegram was slightly optimistic. The school would not welcome its first students until four years later, in 1953. But few disagreed with the sentiment of the missive, that this new deaf school might indeed be the finest in the land. From the main entrance, the campus had sweeping views of the San Gabriel Mountains, snowcapped in winter. The school's low-slung redbrick classrooms and administrative buildings were spread across the gently sloping grounds. It had one of the few swimming pools in the city of Riverside. Visitors would sometimes call the campus the "country club" of state agencies. The dormitories would eventually be known as the cottages, adding to the feel of a resort. Surrounded by citrus groves, it was the furthest thing from the gray institution that the school's advocates had feared.

The school would field its first football team in 1956, the year that Elvis Presley released his first hit single, "Heartbreak Hotel." It was also the year that President Dwight D. Eisenhower would sign a law creating an interstate highway system, forever changing the way Americans lived and traveled and creating a new society based around cars. Nowhere was this more evident than in the growing sprawl that spanned Los Angeles to Riverside.

In the decades after CSDR opened its doors, Riverside would change dramatically from the bucolic, genteel city of plantations rimmed by the growers' mansions. The orange groves would be replaced by strip malls and sprawling housing tracts. "You could make more money selling homes than you could oranges," said Rusty Bailey, a Riverside-born army helicopter pilot who would later serve as a council member and mayor of the city.

The irrigated water would remain crucial, but it would be redeployed for lawns and shrubs and swimming pools. The city of Riverside would swell sixfold, to 300,000 people, by 2022. The region would become known as the birthplace of fast food, with the first McDonald's taking root in neighboring San Bernardino County. Freeways would dissect the region, and car culture would bring with it a choking smog.

Southern California grew to become the country's leading hub for cargo coming in from Asia, the television sets, cars, and plastic toys that would drive the American consumer economy. And Riverside and San Bernardino Counties, together known as the Inland Empire, would play a major role. Mile-long freight trains, the ones that Phillip could hear from the Target parking lot, rumbled past CSDR incessantly. The number of warehouses in the Inland Empire went from 234 in 1980 to more than 4,000 four decades later. From the air, the area looked like a patchwork of white rectangles, one billion square feet of warehouse space.

All this was the Riverside that the California School for the Deaf inhabited as the 2021 football season got under way. The school, which runs from preschool through the twelfth grade, had an enrollment of close to four hundred students in 2021, including a dozen infants who came for child care and early sign-language instruction.

There are remnants of the glory days of the navel orange empire, a revitalized downtown and a state park honoring citrus trees. But they are framed today by the new Riverside, a mosaic of air-conditioned ranch homes, auto dealerships, and those countless warehouses, all strung together by tangled ribbons of freeway.

Vincent Moses, a Riverside historian whose writing is filled with nostalgia, quotes Joni Mitchell: "They paved paradise and put up a parking lot."

4

A Taste of Victory

The puking of Hell Week gave way to more productive practices during the four weeks of the preseason. And as the team prepared for the first game, a Thursday in early September, the players were relieved when evening temperatures dipped into the seventies, perfect football weather. The game was well timed: three days later it would reach 107 degrees in Riverside.

As the home team, the Cubs wore their scarlet-red uniforms, including red pants with a white stripe down the side, and gray helmets. A group of upperclassmen, the stars of the team, had colluded in the equipment room to select their numbers. Felix Gonzales chose No. 1. Enos Zornoza, a senior who played both wide receiver and cornerback, chose 2. Jory Valencia was 3. And Trevin, the quarterback with whom the success of the team seemed destined to rise or fall, was 4. It wasn't complicated for opposing teams to scout which players they needed to worry about. The Cubs had made it easy for them: 1, 2, 3, 4.

The visiting team was Noli Indian, a hearing school an hour southeast of Riverside and located on the Soboba Indian reservation, just over the San Jacinto Mountains from the desert oasis of Palm Springs. All students at Noli were members of federally registered Native tribes in the area. The Noli Indian Braves were a small team with some very big players, including a lineman who weighed 300 pounds and two others pushing 250.

The Braves' head coach, Jesse Aguilar, had been in the job only three weeks. He also served as the school's counselor. Football, as he saw it, was a coping skill, a way to teach leadership and discipline to his players, many of whom came from broken families and in some cases had a parent serving a long prison sentence. Like the Cubs, the Braves considered themselves underdogs. Sometimes when Noli played away games in remote areas, the announcers would refer to them as the Indians, not the Braves, an error that rankled the team.

Aguilar had low expectations as the season got under way. Most of his players were freshmen and sophomores, and because of the pandemic they had never played in a game before.

The last time the two teams had met, before the pandemic, the Braves had come from behind to beat the Cubs in overtime, 20–14. This time, from the very start, was decidedly more lopsided. Enos Zornoza ran back the first kickoff for a touchdown. Then a bad exchange on Noli's first possession between the center and the quarterback caused the Braves to fumble the ball. The Cubs scooped it up, and on the first play on offense Trevin Adams launched a forty-yard pass to Enos for another score. Two touchdowns in less than a minute.

The game proceeded this way for all four quarters, feeling more like a preseason scrimmage. The Cubs scored on every possession they had the ball. They scored a pick six. They scored on the ground and in the air. They blocked a punt. The defense stopped Noli's runners in their tracks, gang-tackling a jumbo running back when they needed to. From the sidelines, Coach Aguilar watched his team being dismantled. He was impressed with the Cubs' timing, with how Trevin, the quarterback, and his receivers seemed to be in sync, even on routes that required higher levels of precision.

The game went very quickly, and the final score, 68–0, was a surprise to everyone involved.

"Are we that good?" Christian Jimenez, a Cubs lineman, asked himself.

The Cubs had spread the ball around. Although Nos. 2 and 4, Zornoza and Trevin Adams, had scored three touchdowns each, it had not been a two-man show. Three other players scored, too, including Phillip Castaneda.

Impressed with his tackling abilities, the coaches had put Phillip in as a starter on defense but not offense. As a newcomer, he was still struggling to learn the offensive playbook. But in the fourth quarter, with the Cubs ahead by so much, they sent Phillip in as running back. On a screen pass, Phillip unzipped the field to the goal line, his 130-pound body flying past the Noli defensemen twice his size. When he reached the end zone, he turned around and saw that the play was called back by a holding penalty. On the very next snap, the coaches called for him to get the ball again. The second-string quarterback, Kaden Adams, Trevin's brother, pitched the ball back to Phillip. Initially uncertain where to run, Phillip slammed into his own quarterback. Sports commentators sometimes talk about a running back bouncing to the outside. Phillip Castaneda had literally bounced off his own teammate, run around the edge of the defense, and dodged two tackles. Displaying his speed and shiftiness, he made it to the end zone again. As a rookie on the team, the homeless running back had notched a touchdown in his very first game.

The coaches were unsure what to make of their runaway victory against Noli. For Coach Adams the game represented a personal milestone as a father: it was the first time he had coached both of his boys, Trevin and Kaden, on the same team. Both boys had inherited a passion for the game, and both were integral to the success of the Cubs.

But it was too early in the season to draw any conclusions. And the players were still not in optimal shape. Kaveh Angoorani, the defensive coordinator, had been confident before the game that the Cubs would win against Noli. But not by *that* much.

After the final whistle, Coach Aguilar assembled his players on the visitors' side of the field for a postgame breakdown. "If you guys really want to know what a team looks like, look across the field," Aguilar remembers telling his young players. "That is discipline. You guys might be mad right now, but you are only freshmen and sophomores. Work hard for two or three years and you guys will look like that."

.   .   .

The Cubs had blown out a team much bigger than them. This was partly the nature of eight-man ball, where one missed tackle can result in a touchdown. Eight-man, as one commentator put it, is football with basketball scores, football on steroids. The game is breathless, punishing, and more dynamic. A seeming blowout can become a close game within minutes.

The eight-man league had been created in 1974 in California for small, often rural schools that "didn't have the facilities or the money," said John S. Dahlem, a former president of the Southern Section of the California Interscholastic Federation, the governing body for high school sports in the state. "They were out in the boonies."

Some coaches called it iron-man football, because players were often required to constantly hustle on both offense and defense in eight-man ball. Dahlem came to admire the game for its speed and action. Eight-man required agility. "You better be able to tackle,"

Dahlem said. "There are going to be 230-pounders out there, but they are not the star players, because they just can't run and keep up. It's a fast game with high scores. And that's why a lot of people really love eight-man. It's just pure," Dahlem said. "It's pure football."

5

Hearing with Your Eyes

It goes without saying that being deaf in a hearing world can be challenging.

But there are also times when it is inconvenient to be hearing. Ask anyone straining to understand their friends at a loud bar.

Ambient noise is not a problem for deaf signers. Deaf scuba divers can effortlessly have conversations with each other underwater. Deaf workers in printing plants or engine rooms can shrug off the noise that hearing workers might find painful and debilitating. And in football, as anyone who has sat through an ear-splitting Seattle Seahawks home game can attest, noise is a weapon, the infamous twelfth man. Make a stadium loud enough and you can bring a well-run offense to its knees, leaving players unable to communicate their next moves and intimidated by the sustained roar. The Cubs, by virtue of their deafness, had the noise weapon neutralized. Thomas Edison, the inventor who helped usher in the modern age of electricity and introduced the world to lightbulbs and the record player, was profoundly hard of hearing for most of his life. Deafness, he was once quoted as saying, gave him "intensive thoughts and concentration."

For Trevin Adams, the Cubs' quarterback, deafness was all he ever knew. He hadn't thought much about the advantages that deafness could bring until he was asked about it. He reasoned that he could stay focused, not affected by his hearing opponents' trash talk, not distracted by jeering spectators. And any efforts by opposing teams to draw the Cubs offside with a so-called hard count would be futile.

"I can't hear their fans, the crowds, or the heckling," Trevin said. "Trash talk. I can't hear it. They can get in my face and tell me anything. We just move on and play our game. It doesn't change our vibe."

It's human nature to categorize. Deafness is often lumped together with other disabilities, like blindness or people who use wheelchairs. In a word association game, a hearing person might casually think of braille when someone mentions deafness. The two have nothing to do with each other, of course, but state governments have been putting blind and deaf students in the same schools for many decades, as with the Arizona State School for the Deaf and the Blind, to give just one example.

What the players and coaches on the Cubs seemed to demonstrate was that deafness as a disability was in a category of its own. Some deaf activists even question whether deaf people should be called disabled. And they have a point: On the campus of a deaf school, who is more disabled, the person who knows American Sign Language and can communicate effortlessly with students and staff? Or the person with perfect hearing who does not know ASL? Deafness, unlike a physical handicap, is essentially a language barrier with the hearing world.

Coach Adams had a very practical attitude toward deafness. Deaf people have four senses, not five, so in that way it's a disability, he reasoned. Before each Cubs game, an interpreter for the team would remind the referees that the players would not be able to hear the whistle. The refs would need to remember to be quick in waving their hands when the play was over.

But Keith Adams was a passionate believer that deafness was not an obstacle on the football field. "It's not going to stop us. In terms of attitude, you make the best of it. It's not something we are going to cry about. There is no woe is me. Going out there in the real world, life is tough. We are going to have a little more adversity. But those are the cards that we were dealt. And you just have to work harder." These were words that could have been spoken by a basketball player who was shorter than his opponents. Or a bicyclist in the Tour de France who did not have the same lung capacity as his competitors.

One seeming challenge for deaf players was the snap count. Over the years, football coaches at CSDR had devised various schemes to replace the traditional "Ready, Set, Hike!" used in the hearing world. One coach who arrived at the school in the 1960s introduced a system where someone on the sidelines would bang a large bass drum. The players could feel the vibrations of the drum and would move on the first, second, third, or fourth beat—whatever had been prearranged. The coach, Pete Lanzi, a retired NFL player who had been drafted by the New York Giants soon after World War II, led the Cubs for nearly a quarter of a century, from 1961 to 1985. Lanzi was remembered as one of the better football coaches at CSDR, but even his tenure would end in a losing record, a combined 76 wins, 124 losses, and 5 ties.

Scott Raymer, a former CSDR student who played guard and defensive end under Lanzi, said he enjoyed watching opposing teams trip over themselves with the drum snaps. "The hearing players didn't know what drum beat to go on, whether it was two beats or three beats. It would confuse them and they would jump offsides," Raymer said.

Keith Adams, who coached the team for two seasons starting in 2005 and then began a second stint in 2017, experimented with the drum. But his players on the sidelines would bang it so hard it would often break. He abandoned the system in favor of a silent count: the quarterback would clap his hands rhythmically, and the center would look through his legs and then snap the ball. All the other players would wait until they saw the ball move.

Adams took pride that the Cubs were rarely penalized, on offense or defense, for moving before the ball was snapped.

"You're deaf," he would joke with his players. "There's no excuses. Just watch the ball!"

After a defensive lineman jumped offside in practice, he pointed out that a few of his players had some residual hearing, meaning that they could hear some sounds very faintly. They might jump when they heard what they thought was an opposing quarterback calling for the ball. So the problem, he joked, was not that these linemen were deaf. It's that they weren't deaf enough.

The clapping system worked well, but it required a high degree of visual synchronization. Part of that came naturally: deaf players were more accustomed to taking visual cues. But in the early weeks of practice, Coach Adams would also submit the team to repeated drills until they developed a unified rhythm. As part of their warm-ups, players would line up on the field, four across. As the quarterback, Trevin would lead the drills and start by clapping, then transition to jumping jacks, then fold into a fighting stance. In the early rounds of the drill, some players failed to follow along. So they did it again. And again. Until they achieved visual synchronicity.

"Hearing teams, all they need is to hear is 'one, two, three,'" Adams said after one practice where he made the team repeat the drill a dozen times. "But for us we don't have that. We need to rely on our visual skills and get everyone on the same page. Hearing teams might have that advantage. But we can make up for it with our visuals."

George Veditz, a deaf pioneer who created a film archive of American Sign Language in the early twentieth century, once described the deaf as "the people of the eye." Science more recently has backed this notion in spades. Research over the last three decades has shown that those who are born profoundly deaf can, on average, see better than hearing people in some specific ways. This is because the brain adjusts to deafness by reorganizing itself. Elissa Newport, a professor at Georgetown University who has devoted her career to understanding this so-called neural plasticity, says people who are deaf from birth have been shown to have a broader field of vision. "Metaphorically, the eyes are trying to do what the ears do," she said. In a number of studies, researchers monitored the brain activity of deaf and hearing subjects as they carried out tests of their vision. The tests roughly resembled the ones routinely used at the eye doctor's office, where patients are told to press a button when they see small flashing lights at different spots. Deaf people were found to perform faster and better than their hearing counterparts at detecting the movement of objects in their peripheral vision. David Corina, a professor at the Center for Mind and Brain at the University of California, Davis, has been involved in a number of studies that showed this heightened eyesight. People who are deaf from birth, Dr. Corina says, have what is called enhanced perception of biological movement. In layman's terms, this means they are better at picking up on the movement of people around them. The world thinks of deafness as hearing loss, Dr. Corina notes. But there is also "deaf gain."

The gain for the Cubs was having a more complete vision of the playing field. At practices, they readily noticed when someone was trying to get their attention, even if they were looking somewhere else. Benjamin Bahan, a professor of deaf studies at Gallaudet University, notes that hearing people tend to pay attention to what is directly in front of them because the responsibility of monitoring what lies on the periphery is left to the ears. Deaf people, by contrast, "learn to read the world for sound," Bahan said.

It takes a lot more than just enhanced peripheral vision to win a championship. Deaf players at CSDR, after all, had been trying since 1956 without success. But this visual acuity was an advantage that they had to exploit. The neural differences meant that players had not only a potentially wider view of activity on the playing field. They could also react more quickly to an opposing team's moves. Milliseconds count in football.

.   .   .

The Cubs had another weapon in their arsenal: American Sign Language. They were able to sign to one another from across the field, beyond the distances over which voice might easily carry.

Football in one crucial respect has been a game of hand signals—by referees—for nearly a century. The hand signals that are now so familiar to football fans began at a 1929 college game between Syracuse and Cornell, according to a history compiled by the National Football League's officiating division. Radio announcers had asked the referee at the game to use a handful of gestures so that they could quickly relay the call to listeners. Previously, referees had simply shouted the calls, a system that had frustrated the announcers and the thousands of fans who often had to guess what the call was. The hand gestures were subsequently adopted by NFL referees, and today referees in the league have a repertoire of more than thirty-five gestures. Over the years, many college and professional teams have also developed their own gestures to call in their plays.

But the Cubs, in contrast to their hearing opponents, had something different and far more sophisticated: an entire language to draw on. It allowed them to speed up the game when they needed to. On many high school football teams, the quarterback runs to the sidelines after each play to get instructions on the next play from the coach. It's a time-consuming routine. The Cubs were able to skip the huddle and quickly set up at the line. Then the players looked to the sidelines for instructions that their coaches signed to them. The system had some similarities to the air-raid offense that some colleges use in that it was fast and breathless, allowing the Cubs to tire out defenses and limit their substitutions.

One of the Cubs' opponents once tried to exploit for their own benefit the Cubs' reliance on sign language. In his first stint as coach, Keith Adams played a team from Malibu that brought a deaf interpreter along to intercept their plays. From then on, Adams decided to encrypt the signs so that even those who knew sign language would not understand what the coaches were saying.

In Adams's new coded system, "Rams" signaled a play to the right. It is signed by running one's hand along the side of the head, mimicking horns. "Lions" signaled a play to the left and is signed by running one's hand across the top of the head, as if combing a lion's mane.

Encrypted or not, the signing between coaches and players on the Cubs was a spectacle, and a distraction, for teams unaccustomed to it. It tended to draw the eyes of opposing teams before the snap, and in the 2019 season, Coach Adams had built a trick play around it. With his offense set on the field, the quarterback at the time, Dylan Eveland, would begin signing with Coach Adams on the sidelines and walked in his direction. It looked as if he were getting instructions, but it was a decoy. As the ASL conversation with the sidelines continued, the ball was snapped to a fullback, who then tossed it to Felix Gonzales. Felix heaved the ball down the field to Eveland for a touchdown. It was one of Keith Adams's prouder moments.

"It was awesome," Adams said.

6

On a Roll

High school football games often begin with an informal ritual. As the teams warm up on opposite sides of the field, players shoot furtive glances to their opponents, sizing them up. The Cubs usually came across as small and somewhat skinny, a team that had not spent much time in the weight room. This was an accurate perception. The coaches and players had been locked out of the athletic facilities for much of the pandemic, and to Galvin Drake's dismay the Cubs players had not taken up a rigorous weight-training schedule since the season began.

They were, on the whole, a team that did not send vibes of intimidation by their size. Felix Gonzales wowed spectators with his aerial gymnastics as he brought down passes. But he was only five feet, eight inches tall. Christian Jimenez, a co-captain of the team and the leader among linemen, was five feet, ten inches. Jory Valencia, the tallest of the starting players, was six feet three but looked like a string bean.

The Cubs made up for this size deficit with fearlessness and physicality on the field. Opposing coaches never failed to mention how hard-hitting they were. They also had speed.

On a kickoff early in the 2021 season, Felix Gonzales caught the ball at the fifteen-yard line, blasted past one defender who tried to drag him down by his jersey, fully spun around 360 degrees to shed another tackler, and finished his run beyond midfield. Later in the same game, he ran another kickoff back from deep near his own end zone, sprinted up the middle, shed two tackles, and outran a third defender, raising the ball in the air once he reached the end zone. He was by far the fastest player on the team. His time in the forty-yard dash, 4.6 seconds, was respectable even by college and NFL standards.

Trevin Adams, stockier than Felix, had a different style of running. His philosophy seemed to be that the shortest distance between two points was straight through the chest of a defender. In the deaf metaphor of the window and the door, Trevin believed in smashing through both. He would secure the ball against his body, lower his pads, and crash forward. Trevin had the same built-like-a-tank look of his father, Coach Adams. Galvin Drake called Trevin a "warrior."

Hitting hard on the football field was something that came naturally to Trevin. Eric Zomalt, a former safety in the NFL for the Philadelphia Eagles, watched Trevin play in a youth league when Trevin was nine years old. Trevin and Zomalt's son were on the same team. "Sometimes you have to teach kids to get over their fear of contact," Zomalt said. "But other kids bite as puppies." He put Trevin in the latter category. "He was fearless," Zomalt said. "He had no hesitation at all to go full speed. He didn't shy away from anything."

In the early parts of the Cubs' games, defenders would see Trevin running toward them and square up for a tackle. But as the game wore on, they would tend to shy away, bruised from the constant contact. A big part of the Cubs' playbook was this Trevin-as-locomotive play, the quarterback keeper. Opposing teams saw Trevin as the classic dual threat, very capable of passing and running.

Carol Adams, Trevin's mother, would watch the games and wince as her son launched himself against opposing players. He clearly reveled in the contact.

"I have no idea where that comes from," she said after one particularly hard-hitting game. Then she answered the question herself: probably from her husband, who was known in his high school playing days to be fast and fearless. "I get butterflies in my stomach," Carol said about watching her son play. "I always think, 'Maybe I need to have a drink.'"

Carol Adams jokes that she becomes a football widow every fall. In the 2021 season, she felt it even more intensely. Her husband, Keith, was the head coach, her eldest son, Trevin, the star quarterback, and her younger son, Kaden, the backup quarterback. The sport swallowed up the family's days, nights, and weekends. Afternoons were dedicated to football practice, and after dark her husband and two boys were often buried in their laptops, watching game film, texting and emailing with other coaches or players. Even dinners at the Adams house often veered into discussions of football, maybe a play that the boys were cooking up, maybe a highlight they shared on their phones. From August through November, Carol Adams knew it was pointless to try to make social plans for the family. That is not to say she didn't enjoy it. Carol Adams was perhaps the team's most faithful fan. She might cringe at Trevin's get-out-of-my-way running style, but come game night, she was always close to the sidelines, her face shining with maternal pride.

Trevin's improvised runs as quarterback helped the Cubs paper over some of their deficiencies, especially their weak offensive line. In a game a third of the way through the season, Trevin offered a demonstration of how he could turn around a play that looked dead on arrival. When he received the snap, he was immediately confronted by a blitzing defender. With a stiff-arm, he shed the tackle and then, bolting upfield, dodged two more defenders. On the way up the left side of the field, passing beside his cheering teammates and coaches on the sidelines, he shrugged off two more diving tackles. And with ten yards to go before the goal line, he dipped his shoulder and barreled into a defensive back. Another defender missed a leaping tackle, flying past Trevin. In the span of a single play, Trevin had eluded nearly every player on the field. He was not the fastest runner on the Cubs—his average was five seconds in the forty-yard dash—but he had an elusiveness and a leather-skinned toughness that made him the leading rusher on the team.

No one hit harder on the team than Trevin, except maybe Cody Metzner, who played running back, linebacker, and nose-guard. Metzner, who could bench-press around 215 pounds, had a distinctive walk, looking as if he had just slugged someone in a bar fight and was now casually strutting into the night. It was a deceptive appearance. He might look and walk like a brute, but Cody was one of the higher-achieving student athletes on the team, taking advanced math and AP English. After college, he hoped to go into software engineering. Putting that academic prowess aside, Cody Metzner described his football philosophy this way: "I want to use my muscle. I want to make them scared of me."

On a third down and four in a game against Hesperia Christian, a school located in the high desert north of Riverside, Metzner, who was playing linebacker, succeeded in terrifying his opponents. The opposing quarterback pitched the ball back to a small but quick running back. Metzner met the runner at the line, lowered his shoulders, and entirely lifted the player off the ground, slamming him to the turf. The hit seemed to defy the laws of physics. There was an action without any reaction. It resembled the crashes that carmakers use to test head-on collisions. On the next play, fourth down, the quarterback handed the ball off to the same running back, who ran to the opposite side of the field, the side where he had a better chance of avoiding Cody Metzner. The runner managed to get the first down but then was met by Felix, who hit him with enough force that the running back spun around like a helicopter blade, thumping onto the turf after a full rotation. Felix, although much slighter in stature, knew how to hit, too.

Some deaf athletes draw a link between deafness and physicality. Peter Leccese, the athletic director at the Indiana School for the Deaf who also serves as assistant coach on their varsity football team, argues that football is a tactile sport and deaf society is also very tactile; getting someone's attention can often mean tapping on their shoulder, for example. But Leccese has also seen another pattern among his players over the years. Football for them, he said, is a release valve, especially for those who were born into hearing families who had trouble communicating with their own parents and siblings.

"Being a deaf person, it's not always easy," Leccese said. "It builds up a lot of frustration. We have all these barriers. Sometimes those boys feel like football is a good way to release all that frustration, all that energy. I see that really often with our deaf kids who have no communication access at home. They do well in football because they are able to express all that energy into their playing."

On the Cubs that energy was funneled into a common cause, a mutual mission to win. The word that came up again and again was "brotherhood." What does it mean to have a deaf brotherhood? For the Cubs, it meant that when they went out into the world together, they were distinct, something akin to members of their own ethnic group. It meant they looked out for one another. They communicated in a different language; they had their own jokes.

It is sometimes said that blindness separates you from things while deafness separates you from people. The aphorism needs a crucial caveat. Deafness does not separate deaf people from one another. It brings them together. The players on the Cubs faced the same basic challenges in a hearing world, whether it was ordering a meal at a fast-food restaurant or enduring the gaze of passersby as they signed to one another.

Inside the fence that ringed CSDR, they were at home in language and culture. It was a feeling of belonging that was amplified in the locker room and on the playing field. Football players at any high school share the bond of brothers in combat. For the Cubs it was an even tighter bond. The team was a vehicle for them to make a statement to an outside world that so often misunderstood them.

.   .   .

Felix Gonzales knew what it meant to be misunderstood. It was a powerful sentiment. It propelled him, like jet fuel. When he was nine years old, he pestered his mother to let him play football. She resisted at first, but Felix was the most athletic of her seven children, and he kept on asking. She signed him up to play in a local Pop Warner league near their home in Harbor City, a working-class neighborhood not far from the port of Long Beach. They lived in the end unit of a two-story pale-yellow apartment building just off a wide boulevard that had donut shops, a palm reader, a topless bar, and a raft of fast-food restaurants.

Felix was the only deaf kid on the team, and the experience was forever seared into his memory. The team's coach would try to give him instructions and then become frustrated when Felix didn't understand them. "The coaches yelled at me more than the other kids," Felix said. "They thought I was clueless."

At nine years old, he turned to YouTube and the internet for tutorials on playing his positions, tight end and linebacker. He studied how players moved, their footwork, the angles that they took on the field. It helped him raise his skill level. But it did nothing to bridge the communication problem with his coach. He remembers being yanked out of games, his coach yelling, "Get out! Get out!" and then standing helplessly for a dressing-down on the sidelines. He could see the anger on his coach's face but could not understand the words.

Delia, Felix's mother, remembers her son returning home after practice, going straight to his room. He wept. He told her he wanted to quit.

When he was in seventh grade, Felix transferred from his local public school to CSDR and met his gym teacher, Keith Adams. Coach Adams encouraged him to join the middle school football team. Felix resisted at first, the bitter memories of playing on the hearing team a few years earlier still fresh. He had also heard that the team was, in his words, "pretty crappy."

But Coach Adams, who had seen what a gifted athlete Felix was, persuaded him with promises of glory.

"Trust me, if you play football with these guys, you are going to get to the championship," Felix remembers Coach Adams saying. Felix joined the team, and in eighth grade the middle school Cubs went on to achieve an 8-0 record.

"That was the first time that I played on a deaf team," Felix said. "It felt good. It was an instant bond. I was surprised at how easy it was to communicate. I didn't even have to think about it."

In high school, Felix was a nonconformist. He was the only player on the Cubs with visible tattoos. He experimented with hair dyes and once had a smiley face shaved into the back of his head. He would arrive at team meetings late and sit in the back of the room snacking. But he knew how to balance individuality with teamwork.

"Finally, I had a connection," he said about playing for the Cubs. "That was when I fell in love with football."

Younger players looked to him as a role model. He was an enormously talented football player. On offense and defense, he seemed to have a sixth sense of where the ball was, pivoting in midair to find it. In many games, he would lead the team both in receptions and in tackles. The team's roster listed every player's position: quarterback, linebacker, safety, and so on. Felix Gonzales was described simply as "athlete."

7

Stamina

The powerhouses of California football tend to be large Catholic schools like Mater Dei and St. John Bosco, both of which consistently rank in the top teams in the country in eleven-man ball. They have stadiums fit for medium-sized colleges, specialized coaching staffs who communicate during games with headsets, and state-of-the-art weight rooms, and some of their games are nationally televised.

The Cubs' opponents, by contrast, were typically small Protestant schools that display varying degrees of competitiveness. The games in the first half of the 2021 season were against a handful of these Christian schools scattered across the high deserts and valleys of Los Angeles, Riverside, and San Bernardino Counties.

In the first two of these games, the Cubs won by wide margins. But those runaway victories seemed to be a reflection of how weak their opponents were as much as of how well the Cubs were playing. In a game against Southlands Christian, a school in the San Gabriel valley east of Los Angeles, bad snaps flew over the quarterback's head repeatedly. The game was called off in the second quarter after a number of Southlands players were injured. It felt like an act of mercy. The score was already 46–0.

But at Calvary Chapel, a school about halfway between Los Angeles and Riverside, the Cubs had their first nail-biter.

From the opening minutes of the game, the Cubs were uncharacteristically out of sync. Trevin Adams was sacked on the very first play. The Calvary defenders burst through the Cubs' offensive line as if it were made of rice paper. Trevin tried a long pass that landed a full two yards beyond the reach of his intended receiver, Jory Valencia. The third play was a muffed snap that forced Trevin to dive onto the turf and smother the loose ball. It was a three-and-out for the Cubs, a rarity, and made worse by a long snap to Felix Gonzales, who had to scramble for the ball before punting it away.

The Cubs turned things around, and by halftime they were winning 38–19. But as the second half wore on, they slowed down. They had their hands on their hips in between plays as they tried to catch their breath. When they made tackles, they got up off the ground slowly. With fatigue came sloppiness. Phillip Castaneda dropped a screen pass. On defense, Trevin missed a tackle that led to a Calvary touchdown. He had the runner in his grasp but just let go, something he almost never did. On a later series, Jory and Trevin got run over by the Calvary quarterback. It was their turn to be trucked.

With just minutes left in the game, the score was Cubs 66, Calvary 57. Calvary had the ball on a fourth down with two yards to go. A Calvary wide receiver caught a screen pass but was tackled inches short of the first-down marker. All the Cubs needed to do to win was hold on to the ball and get a first down.

The Cubs ran down the clock with three running plays but were still short of the first. On fourth down and five, Trevin dropped back, and the porous Cubs' offensive line again let through the rush. With a defender in his face, Trevin threw a pass that flew a dozen yards before sinking to the feet of Jory Valencia. Jory saved the day, scooping up the poorly thrown ball inches before it hit the turf, leaning over to catch the pass the way a shortstop might snag a bouncing grounder. Jory was one yard beyond the first-down marker. The game was over.

The Cubs had won their first close call of the season. They had displayed resilience. But they had betrayed their lack of conditioning and stamina. On the other hand, Calvary was a good team. They would end the season 6-3. The Cubs had shown they could compete at a higher level.

After the game, even though it had been a squeaker, Keith Adams was increasingly optimistic that they would go all the way to the playoffs. He was one step closer to a dream he had been chasing since boyhood, proving that dominance in football had nothing to do with a player's ability to hear.

8

The Sound of the Sun

There is the California of the popular imagination, the beaches and palm trees, Hollywood and Silicon Valley. And then there is Stockton.

As you travel east from the edge of the Pacific Ocean, under the Golden Gate Bridge, past the skyscrapers of San Francisco, beside the oil refineries at Richmond and Benicia and along the curving, watery tendrils at the outer limits of the San Francisco Bay, you reach, sixty miles inland, a flat expanse of a city built on the alluvial soils of the San Joaquin delta. At Stockton, one of California's great rivers, the San Joaquin, meets the wider world, a connection point between Pacific Rim commerce and the Central Valley. A ship carrying palm oil from Malaysia can traverse the ocean, sail across the San Francisco Bay, and snake its way right up to the Stockton city limits.

In the summer of 1975, Linda and Roger Adams pulled in to Stockton in a U-Haul, eager to find a place to settle down with their two boys, Kirk, four years old, and Keith, two. Roger knew he could find work as a bail bondsman in Stockton, and the couple hoped they could afford to buy a home.

They had met in Inglewood, in Los Angeles County, where

Roger had been the captain of the high school football team and Linda had been on a drill team that had once marched in a parade at Disneyland, where she met Walt Disney himself.

After high school they got jobs at pharmacies across the street from each other in Inglewood, Linda at the Sav-On Drugstore, where she worked the ice cream counter, and Roger at Thrifty, where he was a manager.

But they were restless. Both their families had come to California from Oklahoma. And like the Okies of generations past, Roger and Linda wandered the state for their piece of California's vaunted good life, zigzagging from Visalia and Fresno in the Central Valley to San Mateo and Pleasant Hill in the San Francisco Bay Area. They hoped for something more permanent in Stockton.

At different times in its history, Stockton has been a center of world-changing inventions and a magnet for the intrepid. The soft, flood-prone agricultural lands around the city spurred the development of the track wheel system, the heavy-duty, all-terrain belts used on bulldozers, snowmobiles, and tanks. The system would be perfected in Stockton by the co-founder of a company that would later be called Caterpillar.

The city got its start as the launching pad for prospectors from around the globe during the gold rush. They came from Europe, China, and Australia and set out toward the gold-flecked riverbanks of the Sierra Nevada, the iconic mountain range that rises from the valley floor a few dozen miles from Stockton. What had been the land of the Native Yokuts was transformed into a muddy city of mining supply shops, Chinese gambling parlors, and opium dens.

Yet despite gilded beginnings, the city has never quite lived up to its potential, suffering in some neighborhoods from near-Appalachian poverty. Stockton, says Michael Fitzgerald, a long-time columnist at the Stockton *Record,* suffers from "curious invisibility." A city that is one of the most diverse in California and the United States—a mix of whites, Latinos, Blacks, Chinese, Native Americans, Sikhs, Vietnamese, Cambodians, and many others—has one of the starkest legacies of segregation and real estate redlining. In the first two decades of the twenty-first century, the city would become notorious for one of the largest municipal bankruptcies in the United States and as one of the epicenters of foreclosure.

Well before that turmoil, Linda and Roger Adams settled into a ranch home on Dorchester Way in the heart of a newly built quint-essential California development of cul-de-sacs, fenceless front yards, and homes that were only a dozen feet apart. Their neighbors were nurses and plumbers, electricians and teachers.

The aspirations of the residents seemed reflected in the newly minted street names. Two blocks east was Richland Way. No one in the neighborhood was rich just yet. At the end of their street was Hillview Avenue, a name that conjured a desire for elevation in the flat-as-a-pancake city where the closest thing to a hill view was standing on the pitcher's mound at the nearby Lincoln High School, the school where both Kirk and Keith would one day play football.

For Linda, Stockton presented the twin challenges of settling into a new city and dealing with a diagnosis that the couple had received when they were still in Los Angeles and that had shocked them and brought tension into their marriage.

Keith had been around six months old when Linda observed that he was different from his brother.

Kirk, in his infant years, had responded to his mother's reassurances. When he woke up in the mornings, Linda would say, "Okay, Mommy is coming!" and the words would soothe him. With Keith, those maternal exclamations seemed to make no difference. When she told her pediatrician about this, the doctor examined Keith, waved a red ball around, commented that he was already crawling and that he showed signs of being precocious. The doctor dismissed her concerns. "He's very bright," Linda remembered the doctor telling her. "Nothing wrong with him."

Two months later she returned from a trip to Las Vegas with a souvenir, a dinner bell that she had planned to give to an in-law who collected them. As she prepared to gift wrap the bell, she walked behind Keith, who was sitting in his high chair, and jingled it. It was loud. She rang it again. Growing alarm spread inside her when she saw that her son had no reaction to this earsplitting noise. She dropped the bell onto the kitchen floor, where it broke into pieces. And she, too, collapsed, and cried.

"I didn't know anything about deafness," Linda would recall years later.

She brought Keith to a specialized medical center, the John Tracy Clinic in Los Angeles, a nonprofit organization founded by the actress Louise Tracy, wife of the actor Spencer Tracy, in honor of their deaf son. Louise Tracy had discovered their son was deaf when, at ten months old, he did not react to a door slamming shut. What is now known as the John Tracy Center was founded in 1943 to provide resources for parents of deaf children.

Keith, propped up in a special booth, was unresponsive when an audiologist played sounds that emanated from a puppet. A hearing child might be drawn to the puppet as the source of the sounds. The diagnosis came swiftly: Keith was "profoundly deaf."

Linda remembers Roger reacting angrily to the audiologist's findings, seeing deafness as a defect. "It must be from your side of the family," she remembers him saying. Over the next few years, once they had settled into Stockton, it would largely be up to her to navigate her son's deafness, a world very new and daunting to her.

Keith's diagnosis, and its timing, were crucial. Less severe types of deafness might allow a child to hear some speech and thus follow the educational route of a hearing child. But Keith's profound deafness meant that he could hear only extremely loud sounds, like nearby motorcycles or airplane engines.

Profound deafness is in a category of its own, especially for those who are deaf at birth, before the acquisition of language. Profound deafness requires immediate action on the part of parents. It can be dangerous in this way: learning a language is primordial and essential, closely intertwined with the thought process.

Studies in recent decades have shown that without language a child can suffer substantial damage to their cognition and their social lives, according to Elissa Newport, a Georgetown professor who has spent decades studying the brain's acquisition of language. It doesn't matter if it's sign language or a spoken language. Humans are social beings, and learning to communicate is urgent in childhood. In the extreme, language deprivation can cause severe mental handicaps.

Delayed diagnosis of deafness happened very often before hearing tests were made mandatory for newborns in the United States. By the late 1990s, when the first states enacted regulations to mandate hearing tests for newborns, just 20 percent of U.S.-born babies were tested before they were one month old. Today, with testing adopted by all but a handful of states, more than 98 percent of babies receive the tests. For every thousand births in the United States, around two babies are diagnosed with some form of hearing loss. Around one-tenth of those are diagnosed as profoundly deaf.

At the time of Keith's diagnosis in the 1970s the prevailing advice among doctors was to try to teach deaf children speech and lip-reading. The theory put forward by hearing doctors was that children would better integrate into the wider world, unlike with sign language, which would cloister them among the deaf. Sign was, and sometimes still is, portrayed as a kind of last resort for parents.

The Cleveland Elementary School, the public school serving

Linda's area in Stockton, had both the "oral" route of speech and a separate class for children learning to sign. As if to underline the differing approaches, they were in separate buildings. Linda remembers the signing class having a stigma among the parents of deaf children.

"It was as if the dumber kids were the ones who had to learn sign," she said.

A photo of Keith at the time shows a boy with hazel-brown eyes and a helmet of blond hair watching the world around him with a pensive and observant gaze. Wires protrude from his ears. On the advice of doctors, Linda had bought hearing aids in the hope that they might capture any sounds at all. The devices were connected to a box the size of a pocket notebook that hung around Keith's neck. A few years later Keith would put them in a drawer. They were useless to him.

Doctors and therapists offered advice on how Keith might learn to speak. They told Linda to have Keith touch the dishwasher when it was running for "sound awareness." They told her to put Keith's hand on her throat so he could feel the vibrations as she spoke.

She would stretch out words and crouch down to his level so he would see her exaggerated lip movements. "We are going to eeeaaat," she would say.

"Everything you would put before him, you would try to mouth it out so he would know what you were talking about," Linda remembers.

A speech therapist used multicolored Kleenex as a memory tool for different sounds. A blue Kleenex might mean you had to blow outward with certain sounds. A red Kleenex would represent another sound. And so on.

Linda drove Keith to an infant-and-toddler program at Cleveland Elementary, where he joined four or five other deaf children.

During one trip to the school, she nicked the car in front of her while parking, and when she searched out the person who owned the car to tell him she would pay for the damages, he turned out to be the school's sign-language teacher, Dale Delp. The damage was minimal, but this minor traffic accident would later prove to be pivotal for both Keith and Linda.

Going the oral route was a painstaking process. At Cleveland Elementary, she remembers the plaudits Keith received when he learned to say a single sentence, "I want a donut." This one accomplishment had taken months to achieve.

There were certain sentences Linda would repeat over and over. She enunciated with great emphasis "I love you" and remembers Keith responding by pointing to his mother and pointing to himself, acknowledging that he had understood. Progress was very slow. One author on deafness has compared the difficulty for a profoundly deaf person learning spoken English to an American with perfect hearing trying to learn spoken Japanese from inside a soundproof glass cubicle.

But a eureka moment came during a get-together with Linda's sister, Mary, when Keith was three years old. Mary lived in Southern California, where she ran a preschool out of her house. On the advice of a neighbor, she had taken sign-language classes, thinking that it might enhance her teaching skills. Linda and Mary had met at their mother's house in the Central Valley and were serving Keith a snack.

As they stood at the refrigerator, Linda tried, as she had for months, to have Keith lip-read, asking him whether he wanted milk or juice. She stretched out the pronunciation of the words. "Miiiiillllk. Juuuuuuuice." Keith looked on in puzzlement.

Mary took over, using the sign-language vocabulary she had learned at her classes. She signed milk, which is done by squeezing a fist as if milking a cow. And she pointed to the milk. Then she signed juice, which is most commonly signed by swiping a pinkie finger near the edge of one's mouth. She pointed to the juice. Keith immediately responded by replicating the sign for juice.

"Keith's face lit up," Linda said. "Right then I knew we needed to learn sign language."

Linda Adams reached out to Dale Delp, the teacher whose car she had scraped in the school parking lot, and asked if he would be willing to teach sign language to her and anyone else in the community who was interested. Dale agreed on the condition that classes not be held on Wednesday, when he had a church function. Linda then rounded up enough people to justify the cost of holding the class at a local community college.

In the competing philosophies between the oral and the signing routes, Dale Delp was, by the circumstances of his birth, firmly in the signing camp. He was the hearing son of two deaf parents, and sign language was his first language.

While many hearing people at the time saw deafness as a challenge that needed to be overcome, deafness was something normal to Dale. He understood the deaf perspective on the hearing world.

He recalled a deaf middle school student in one of his physical education classes, a very athletic boy who tried to play with the hearing children. Dale had noticed that it was rare for hearing children to reach out to deaf children; maybe one out of twenty-five would approach a deaf student. Sports provided a common activity for the hearing and the deaf, but the athletic deaf boy in his class was still disappointed; the boy lamented the communication barrier between him and the hearing kids, but not in the way that many hearing people might analyze it.

"I wish they were all deaf so I could talk with them," Dale remembers the boy signing.

Dale bristled at the notion that deafness was a handicap that needed to be fixed. Ordained as a pastor in a Pentecostal church, he once ran a deaf ministry and remembers attending an annual conference in Stockton with college students in the 1980s. A visiting minister preached on the importance of healing, and at the end of the sermon the minister encouraged acts of healing. On cue, the hearing college students in attendance gravitated toward Dale's deaf congregation, ready to heal them.

Dale stood up and blocked their way. "Wait a second!" he remembers shouting. He turned to his congregants and signed to them, asking whether they wanted to be "healed." They looked at one another with puzzlement and agreed that they did not.

With the weekly sign-language classes, Dale Delp had opened an entirely new world to Linda Adams—and a new chapter in the relationship with her son. In the era before television shows were captioned, she sat on the floor interpreting programs for Keith. And she became a sign-language tutor for Kirk and her husband.

In January 1982 the family gathered to watch Super Bowl XVI, between the San Francisco 49ers and the Cincinnati Bengals. It was held near Detroit—the first Super Bowl to be hosted in a cold, wintry city. And Keith remembers his father holding a newspaper before the game and showing him an article about it. "My dad was telling me about the teams and that they were going to the Super Bowl. And I thought, what do they mean Super Bowl? What is that?"

It would be an awakening for Keith, a window into a sport that everyone in his family loved. His mother joked that it was destiny for a ten-pound newborn to play football. Keith, who would reach 250 pounds by the time he was a high school sophomore, was already clamoring to play the game at eight years old, begging to play in the same league as his brother, Kirk, two years his senior.

But it was also telling that Keith, despite his interest in football, did not know what the Super Bowl was. A hearing child might have overheard people talking about it. But for a young deaf child in a hearing family there was no way to absorb knowledge by linguistic osmosis. This lack of casual absorption of language is one of the reasons that learning to read is an added challenge for deaf children. Many of the words on the page are brand-new to them.

Reading for Keith was a crucial path of discovery. He and his mother would sit in the living room, where Keith would sign to his mother questions about passages he did not understand.

When he was around nine years old—Linda does not remember his exact age—Keith was reading a book that mentioned the wind rustling through the trees. Rustling? What did that mean? he asked his mother.

Linda explained that when the wind blew, leaves and boughs made a noise. It's a way that hearing people know that a gust of wind is under way, she explained.

Keith absorbed this knowledge and followed up with another question.

"What sound does sunshine make?"

9

Frowned upon by the Gods

The reckoning that Linda Adams had at the refrigerator, the realization that her son was craving language, was a parable for two centuries of tensions among educators over how best to teach deaf students. Sign versus oral has been an enormously bitter clash. Deaf people were more often than not sidelined in these debates, even though the outcomes were crucial to their livelihoods. *Sidelined,* in fact, could be the title of a book on early deaf history.

Studying deaf history, the scholar H-Dirksen Bauman has written, is like chasing the path of a firefly on a dark night. There are brief moments of illumination followed by extended periods of darkness. Because the first known writings by a deaf person did not come until the late eighteenth century, the glimpses into what life was like for deaf people before then almost always came from outsiders, from hearing people.

Like spoken languages, sign languages emerged organically around the globe, independent of one another. For centuries, there has been a lively debate among scholars over whether sign languages preceded spoken ones, whether all humans were once signers before they were talkers. We may never know the answer. In tracking the earliest known sign languages, we rely on fleeting historical accounts, the fireflies in Bauman's example, to cast the dimmest of lights onto the existence of now-disappeared languages.

The ancient Greek philosopher Socrates in the fifth century BC wrote about deaf people who "make signs with the hands, head and the rest of the body." In Ottoman Turkey, European visitors to the Topkapi palace in Istanbul were surprised to see the sultan conversing with his servants in sign language. Tradition held that the sultan must live in silence and seclusion. Deaf courtiers were prized in this environment. Sara Scalenghe, a scholar of Middle East history, writes that one European traveler counted as many as a hundred deaf people signing in the sultan's court and that the language appeared to be carried on for generations.

All available evidence suggests that this relatively elevated place of deaf Ottoman servants was a rare, happy circumstance. For millennia, the world's greatest civilizations, even as they made strides in science, technology, and education, had attitudes toward deafness that ranged from apathy to loathing and abandonment. In many parts of the world, deaf people were barred from inheriting property, prohibited from marrying, and considered unintelligent and less than human. This latter judgment was self-fulfilling: denied access to written languages—and the generational bridge of knowledge that books provided—deaf people were derided as "dumb."

In India, an ancient Hindu legal text, the Manu Smriti, put deaf people in the same category as animals and stipulated that they be denied any rights. Deafness, according to Madan Vasishta, an Indian-born graduate of Gallaudet University, was considered the consequence of sins committed in an earlier incarnation. And deaf people, along with the blind and the "deformed," were to be "despised by the virtuous." The words in South Asian languages for deaf—*bola* in Punjabi, *behra* in Urdu, and *vadhir* in Hindi— were all hurled as insults.

In imperial China, deaf people were technically permitted to marry, inherit property, and have the same rights as hearing people, according to Shu Wan, a scholar who specializes in the study of disabilities in China. But in reality the deaf were often considered unfit for marriage, and deaf children were viewed as an embarrassment to families, denied education, and considered nonproductive members of society. *Peeps into the Deaf World,* a book of vignettes from around the globe that was published in 1917, included this harrowing description: a deaf child in China "is regarded as one upon whom the gods have frowned; he is teased and ill-treated by all the boys in his native village; he is sent out to beg or to gather grass and roots for fuel if his parents are poor, and hidden if the family is one of wealth and influence."

In Europe, despite the ideas of the Enlightenment, the pursuits of knowledge and reason, there was a belief that deaf people were "beyond the reach of the gospel," as one historian put it, not capable of Christian faith. Saint Paul's writings were cited: "Faith comes through hearing." There were exceptions—wealthy families who educated their deaf child, for example. But the vast majority of the deaf lived in a vacuum of public empathy. Sign languages sprang up in deaf communities, and families touched by deafness developed what are known as home signs. In the wider society, however, and especially among the intellectual classes, using gestures to communicate was derided as rudimentary and pantomimic.

Then came what Oliver Sacks, the late neurologist who wrote a book on deafness, *Seeing Voices,* called the "golden period in deaf history." In the decades before the French Revolution, a pioneering French priest who himself had been marginalized by the Church sparked what would prove to be its own revolution in the world of the deaf.

Charles-Michel de l'Epée, scion of a wealthy family who had served in the court of Louis XIV in the early eighteenth century, took an interest in the deaf community in Paris and learned the signs they used to communicate. He established what Harlan Lane, the late scholar of deaf history, called "the first public school for the deaf in the history of the world." That's a claim difficult to definitively prove given the millennia of interactions between deaf and hearing people. But what is certain is that the educational movement that Epée launched in Paris spawned institutions that spread across Europe, to Rome, Amsterdam, Madrid, and Vienna, and beyond. Epée's disciples would ultimately launch two hundred schools for the deaf, including what is today called the American School for the Deaf in Hartford, Connecticut, a school that the Cubs' defensive coordinator, Kaveh Angoorani, would attend a century and a half after its founding in 1817.

Crucially, Epée's work brought about a fundamental change in attitudes toward deafness. Being deaf had long been lumped together with other handicaps and "deformities," in the parlance of the time. But Epée's work demonstrated to the European elites that deaf communities on their own had no inherent disability: they could communicate fluidly with one another in sign. The barrier that existed was when a deaf person interacted with the hearing world.

Epée's movement was first and foremost one of education. But it also carried out what in modern vocabulary might be called marketing, an effort to convince the hearing that deafness, with the right resources, was not an obstacle to knowledge and intelligence. Epée and his successors managed to spark fascination about sign language among the elites of the day, archbishops and emperors. The school held seminars where deaf students and teachers would be quizzed. "What is the difference between desire and hope?" a visitor asked at one of the sessions. The question was directed to Jean Massieu, who had gained a measure of fame as the first deaf teacher at the school. Massieu replied poetically: "Desire is a tree with leaves, hope is a tree in bloom, enjoyment is a tree with fruit."

The network of deaf schools that branched out from France served to spread sign languages in a more systematic way. Contrary to what is often believed among hearing people, the multitude of sign languages in the world are as different from one another as, say, Chinese is from Portuguese. A Japanese signer cannot easily converse with an American one. But when certain sign languages do overlap, it is often because of the pioneering paths of early deaf teachers. One of the teachers at Epée's school in Paris, Laurent Clerc, was persuaded to travel to America by Thomas Hopkins Gallaudet, a Philadelphia-born Protestant minister who had taken on as a mission the education of deaf students. Once in America, Laurent Clerc taught and adapted French sign language, and he and Gallaudet co-founded the Hartford school. Clerc would also co-found Gallaudet University in Washington, D.C., named in honor of Thomas Hopkins Gallaudet and today the world's premier university for deaf students.

The consequence of this Frenchman's pioneering role is that today more than half of the signs in American Sign Language have French roots. This is because one Frenchman—Laurent Clerc—sailed across the Atlantic and brought with him the sign language he had taught at the pioneering school in Paris. American signers are essentially using a derivative of eighteenth-century Parisian sign language. This also means that today French Sign Language and American Sign Language are much closer linguistically than American Sign Language is to British Sign Language, despite the United States and Britain being English-speaking countries and having a shared colonial past. American Sign Language and British Sign Language are mutually unintelligible, as far apart as two unrelated spoken foreign languages.

Perhaps the most important part of Epée's legacy was that it gave deaf communities, for the first time on such a large scale, access to books, to reading and writing, the crucial links to the past and the future. The common, institutionalized sign language developed at Epée's school gave rise to a wider deaf community that could communicate not just through sign but through the

French writing that deaf students learned. This led to milestones like the 1779 publication of one of the first books known to have been written by a deaf person, *Observations* by Pierre Desloges.

The purpose of Desloges's book was to make the case that sign language was the most appropriate way for deaf people to communicate. It was an impassioned plea. "We express ourselves on all subjects with as much order, precision, and rapidity as if we enjoyed the faculty of speech and hearing," Desloges wrote.

He made a persuasive case, but the battle was not won.

.   .   .

Almost exactly a century later, all these advances by the deaf community were rolled back at a meeting that remains today a symbol in the wider deaf world of rules imposed on deaf people without their participation or consent.

The 1880 International Congress of Educators of the Deaf, held in Milan, came to the conclusion that the oral route was the only appropriate path for deaf students. Sign language was banned from schools. This was akin to prohibiting native populations from using their own language, another common practice of the time. Alexander Graham Bell, the inventor whose fascination with the transmission of sound led him to patent the telephone, had a personal stake in the debate. His mother and wife were both deaf, something that helped nurture his interest in acoustics. Bell argued that deaf people should learn to speak, and his influence at the Milan conference helped tip the scales toward the total ban on sign language. It was a catastrophic decision for the deaf community.

The arc of history bends toward a better world, we are told. The late nineteenth century was a time of great scientific strides and great inventions. The automobile, the telegraph, recorded music, and of course Bell's telephone. But for the deaf world, the Milan conference was a 180-degree turn after a century of progress. The arc was broken. By the end of World War I, 80 percent of deaf children in the United States were taught entirely without sign language. The ban on using sign language in classrooms continued well into the twentieth century, and many schools used corporal punishment to enforce it.

In the 1960s, teachers at the California School for the Deaf, Riverside punished students if they used American Sign Language in the classroom. American Sign Language has its own grammar and vocabulary. It is fast and fluid among native signers. The school instead only allowed students to use their fingers to painstakingly mimic the English alphabet and spell out every letter of every word. It was a form of English transcribed onto fingers. A student who wanted to leave the classroom to go to the bathroom might be forced to spell out "M-A-Y I G-O T-O T-H-E B-A-T-H-R-O-O-M." The ASL equivalent, by contrast, would have taken a second or two: making a fist while sliding one's thumb between the index and middle finger, the sign for bathroom.

One of the students who would be punished for using ASL was Ken Watson, a future assistant coach on the Cubs football team.

Watson, who began attending CSDR in 1957, remembers the smell of orange blossoms on the campus. But he also has the sharp memory of being caught numerous times for using ASL and then standing at the blackboard writing "I will not sign in the classroom" five hundred times. ASL was the natural language that he and all his friends used to communicate. But the stigma attached to sign language, a prejudice that dated back millennia, still held sway.

"Whenever the teacher was looking away, we tried to sign to each other, but we had to be really careful about it," he said.

Decades later, as the oldest coach on the Cubs, Ken Watson would witness the success of the CSDR football program. With its all-deaf roster of players and coaches, it was a coda to the oppressive history that deaf people had endured. This all-deaf team had as one of its more potent and unique weapons American Sign Language, the same language that had once been banned across the Western world, the same language Ken Watson had been punished for using as a student at the California School for the Deaf, Riverside.

As recently as 2010, a group of seven doctors and linguistics experts from universities across the country would author a paper that read more like a desperate entreaty to hearing parents on the importance of sign language.

"The development of language is critical to the organization of memory, mastery of cognitive skills such as numeracy and literacy, and many other aspects of cognitive development," they wrote. "High proficiency in a language permits a child to engage in social interactions with family and peers. . . . It is, therefore, critical that a deaf child become a fluent signer."

.   .   .

After she learned sign language, Linda Adams launched into studying to become a special education teacher. The watchword at the time, in the 1980s, was "mainstreaming," the notion that deaf children should be put in classrooms with hearing students. But when a professor in Linda's special education master's program assigned a paper on mainstreaming, Linda took a contrarian tack and wrote a paper titled "When Mainstreaming Is Not Appropriate." She argued that sometimes it was more beneficial for deaf children to be among other deaf children, that it gave them camaraderie and an opportunity to communicate with more fluency. It was as if she was opening a portal to the future, describing the benefits of the all-deaf football team that her son would coach decades later. She remembers her professor telling her how refreshing it was to read that point of view because the other twenty students in the class had parroted the prevailing ideas on the benefits of mainstreaming.

Linda's philosophy carried over into decisions about her son's schooling. Keith Adams, still enrolled in a local public school, had a close friend who had transferred to the California School for the Deaf in Northern California, which had moved from Berkeley to Fremont, also in the Bay Area. The friend had raved about the Fremont school to Keith, and at age twelve he decided he wanted to enroll.

Keith blossomed at Fremont. "Being able to talk to my teachers directly and not going through an interpreter," Keith remembered, "the level of stimulation was much higher." Looking back, he said, he had not clamored for this all-deaf environment earlier because he didn't understand how transformative it would be. "If you've never had candy, why would you even think you want it? You wouldn't until you have a taste of it; then you want to eat candy all day long."

Keith had another reason to enjoy his time at an all-deaf school. He encountered Carol Bella, a fellow student. The two met while acting in a school production of the *Nutcracker* together. Keith Adams performing in a ballet featuring plum fairies is a notion that would bring a smile to the face of anyone who knew him decades later as the passionate, rough-around-the-edges football coach throwing down his clipboard when the Cubs fumbled the ball.

Carol grew up in Antioch, along the San Joaquin River delta, where her grandmother had worked on cannery row, not the one made famous by Steinbeck. This was one closer to San Francisco and was a shipping hub for all the fruits and vegetables harvested in the orchards and farms of the East Bay. Her father's family was Mexican and her mother's Italian. Carol's upbringing was distinct from Keith's in one very crucial way: both her parents were deaf.

Her father had toiled through a particularly difficult life: raised on a ranch, he had been deprived of an education until he was eleven years old. As an adult he worked as a cabinetmaker and died of a heart attack when he was fifty-four.

Keith and Carol started dating when Carol was a sophomore and Keith a junior.

After both graduated from Gallaudet University, Keith and Carol, the high school sweethearts, would marry in Lafayette, California, a San Francisco suburb and a short drive from where Carol grew up in Antioch. They spent a few years in the Bay Area and then moved to Riverside, where both found jobs at CSDR and where they would start a family.

10

The FaceTime Revolution

Keith and Carol were under the impression that their first child would not be deaf. Deafness is often hereditary, and the couple had done tests looking for genetic markers. This was 2005, and the research at the time pointed to a hearing child.

But when Trevin Adams was born on February 11, a doctor came into the hospital room looking grave.

"I'm so sorry, but your child is deaf," Carol remembers the doctor saying. Maybe it was fluid in the ear, he told her. They could test again.

"Don't worry about it," Carol Adams told the doctor. She was not upset that her son was deaf.

Keith was surprised but unfazed. "Hearing or deaf, it didn't make a difference to us," he would say later. "The only important thing is that the child is healthy."

Trevin Adams was born three decades after his parents, but his childhood would seem to be from an entirely different age. American Sign Language was the unquestioned language of communication both at home and in school. And technology had transformed deaf lives.

When his mother was growing up in Antioch in the 1980s, the

family relied on a specialized service that would deliver a projector and films that were captioned. Watching the *Swiss Family Robinson* and *Old Yeller* and being able to read the dialogue was a treat, something that the family did once a month or so. But Trevin could turn on the television and nearly every show was captioned.

When they were dating, Keith and Carol needed devices known as a text telephone/teletypewriter, or TTY, to call each other. If they wanted to call someone hearing, they would type the message into the TTY and an operator would then read it out. It was slow and tedious.

Their son, by contrast, had multiple ways to communicate with his friends, both deaf and hearing. He could text anyone with a mobile phone or use FaceTime and sign with his friends on his iPhone. The classrooms in his school were all equipped with videophones that would flash when a call came in.

The first decade of the twenty-first century was a time of immeasurable change in technology, and it affected the deaf population vastly. When Steve Jobs introduced the iPhone on a San Francisco stage in 2007, he called it "a revolutionary and magical product that is literally five years ahead of any other mobile phone." But in the context of deaf history, he could have easily been talking about a leap of centuries, not years. The introduction of the smartphone was a watershed moment. It has already made it infinitely easier for deaf and hearing communities to communicate with each other. Future technologies promise to bridge the gap even more profoundly: glasses that show the wearer real-time captioning of conversations; an app that translates sign language into text.

By the time Trevin was playing football at CSDR, the chasm that had long existed between the way deaf and hearing people communicated with one another had narrowed dramatically. Trevin and his teammates share videos with one another just as his hearing counterparts do. They watch game film of their opponents on their phones and laptops. They text one another into the night with ideas for plays and strategies to beat their upcoming opponents.

The generational divide was even starker between Trevin and the Cubs' assistant coach Ken Watson, who was born in 1952. Watson dreaded summers because it meant that he would be alone in the family's mobile home park, separated from his deaf schoolmates. Summertime—the time of year that most schoolchildren pine for—was Ken Watson's season of loneliness. The only contact he had with his deaf friends over the summer was exchanging letters through the post office. When John F. Kennedy was assassinated in 1963, Watson was in school and his teacher, learning the news, put her head down on the desk and began crying. The students were in the dark and only fully grasped what had happened when they were allowed to watch television and a counselor interpreted what was being said. At home, Watson had very limited communication with his hearing parents. They had learned only very basic signs. At social gatherings his father would try to shunt his deaf children aside. "He would kind of try to hide us," Watson said.

With two deaf parents, Trevin Adams never had any problem communicating at home. Mealtime was a flurry of signing, often conversations about football. When they went out into the world, Trevin's brother, their hearing sister, and their parents were always one text message away from one another.

Carol Adams has the same concerns that hearing parents have about her children constantly being engrossed in their phones, the addiction of the screens. She sees the younger generation's social muscles weakened by technology, and she tries to fight back. Phones are not allowed at the dinner table. But the good mostly outweighs the bad: the technology, the internet and smartphones, give her children an admission ticket to a much wider world than she experienced. "The access for the kids is amazing," she said.

11

Deafness as a Choice

As summer turned to fall, the Cubs had gained confidence in their skills and their teamwork. They were winning. On the last day of September, halfway through the regular season, the Cubs played another small Christian school, Lutheran High School from La Verne, a city on the eastern edge of Los Angeles County. It was a lopsided game, and at halftime the Cubs were already ahead, 46–0. As the third quarter began, the coaches put in a player who had just joined the team. His name was Dominic Turner, and he stood a little taller than six feet and weighed around 240 pounds, a good deal of it pandemic weight. He had a well-proportioned jawline and brown hair kept in a tight, Ivy League haircut. He had transferred to CSDR a few weeks into the school year and had immediately caught the eye of Keith Adams. Adams wasted no time to make his move.

"You're kind of a big guy; you would be a good lineman," Dominic remembers Adams telling him. Dominic told Coach Adams he didn't like football much. He hadn't grown up watching it—his grandmother who raised him never had it on—and his previous experience trying to play at hearing schools had been an exercise in alienation.

Keith's second son, Kaden, the backup quarterback, was also in the gym class, and he joined in the recruitment effort. Pretty soon, the entire gym class was trying to persuade Dominic to join the team. And it worked. Dominic fired off a text to his grandmother: "Pick me up at 6:00 p.m. I've joined the football team."

Dominic had attended seven different schools in his fifteen years of life, but none had quite worked out. He was a good student, generally getting As and Bs, but as a deaf boy in hearing schools he found his social life frustrating. In elementary school he was rarely invited to parties or birthdays or to friends' homes after school. He was teased because of his deafness.

"They would ask me to say stuff, and then, when I couldn't say it right, when I couldn't produce the words right, that was funny to them and they would laugh," Dominic said. He found himself watching as classmates chatted and played. "I felt so alone. No one was communicating with me at all."

The best word he found to describe how he felt in those schools was "foreigner." It was a powerful sentiment considering that he was anything but foreign to Southern California. Born in Riverside, he spent his childhood there and in Mission Viejo, a city not far from the ocean in Orange County.

In the fall of 2021, after California schools had emerged from their COVID lockdowns, Dominic had made the last-minute decision to try CSDR. It would be his second time: he had attended the school as an infant and kindergarten student. Now he was returning, abruptly, desperate to find a place where he felt more at home. He was leaving his hearing school even as his sophomore year was already under way.

In the game against Lutheran, Dominic took his place on the defensive line, crouched down, and put one hand on the turf, set for his first play. It was a pitch to Lutheran's running back, and as soon as the ball was snapped, Dominic drove the center out of the way and with the help of his fellow lineman Alfredo Baltazar tackled the runner for a loss. Not bad for his very first play in a CSDR uniform. The Cubs went on to win the game, 68–0, and their record improved to 5-0.

After years of searching, Dominic had found his place. Finally, he had this coach and this team where communication wasn't a problem. The pandemic was still raging in the fall of 2021, and the mood in California was one of frustration. But when a visitor asked Dominic how he was enjoying his football season, he did not hesitate. "Very fun," he said. "Very, very fun." He was a "foreigner" in California no more.

Dominic was born profoundly deaf. But later in life his deafness came with an asterisk. At five years old, he underwent an operation to install, under the skin behind his ear, an electronic device known as a cochlear implant. Distinct from hearing aids, which are a set of tiny microphones and speakers that amplify sounds and pipe them into the ear at higher volumes, cochlear implants communicate directly with the brain. They are basically bionic ears. They translate sounds into electrical impulses that stimulate the nerve that connects to the brain stem. The stuff of science fiction only a few decades ago, they allow most deaf people who undergo the operation to hear in varying degrees. For Dominic, whose mother tongue is ASL, which he learned as an infant, the implant gave him a facsimile of hearing and put him in an unusual position. He could switch between the hearing and the deaf worlds at will. He could wake up in the morning and decide whether to have five senses or four. It was something unimaginable to generations before him: it was up to him whether he wanted to hear—or not.

Often, he chose not.

The cochlear implant, a device that would rock the deaf world, was a California invention pioneered by the son of a dentist, William House. House grew up on a ranch in Whittier, a city in Los Angeles County halfway between the coast and Riverside. He attended both dentistry and medical school and was an inveterate tinkerer who seemed to enjoy bucking the medical establishment. He performed one of his first innovations, an experimental surgery to treat the inner-ear affliction called Ménière's disease, on Alan Shepard, the navy test pilot who in 1961 became the first American in space. Ménière's can lead to debilitating vertigo, and Shepard's career had been threatened by bouts of dizziness, tinnitus, and vomiting. When other treatments failed, Shepard secretly traveled to Los Angeles to be treated by House, who at the time was a relatively obscure dentist and researcher publishing papers on his experiments. The surgery was successful, and Shepard went on to join the Apollo 14 mission that lifted off from Cape Canaveral on January 31, 1971, and rocketed to the moon. Shepard became famous for whacking a golf ball using a makeshift six iron in the thin atmosphere on the moon. From space, he spoke to House, who was a guest at Mission Control in Houston. "I'm talking to you through the ear that you operated on!" Shepard said from 230,000 miles away.

At the time of the moon mission, House, already deep into his experiments with cochlear implants, was on the receiving end of heavy criticism. Some doctors believed that sending pulses of electricity through the inner ear could cause irreparable damage. Others simply said the device would not work. One pediatric ear expert was quoted saying there was no "moral justification for an invasive electrode for children." But House persisted, and in 1984 the Food and Drug Administration approved the sale of his device. It was a crude version of what would come later. Patients reported being able to hear doorbells and car horns and muffled speech, sounds like "that of a radio not completely tuned in," House said on the day the FDA announced the approval of the implant. But even in its more primitive form, there was a sense that history was being made with this new product. "For the first time, a device can, to a degree, replace an organ of the human senses," the deputy director of the FDA, Mark Novitch, said at a news conference in Washington when House's invention was introduced. "Soon a device like this may produce an understanding of speech to many for whom even crude sound would have been considered hopeless just a few years ago."

Four decades later, implants have to some extent achieved that goal. Richard K. Gurgel, one of the leading researchers in the field of cochlear implants, estimates that around 95 percent of deaf people are candidates for implants and that the technology employed in the devices has improved by leaps and bounds. In many countries, including Sweden and France, deaf children receive cochlear implants almost as a matter of course. Implants can now be equipped with Bluetooth technology so a person can listen to a podcast or receive a phone call that is directly transmitted through the implant to the brain. Although most devices today consist of two pieces—the part that is embedded under the skin and a part that attaches, by magnet, on top of the skin—future models will be fully implanted and thus invisible to other people.

Crucially, however, cochlear devices do not produce what would generally be considered normal hearing. Ann Geers, a developmental psychologist who has been studying cochlear implants for four decades, says a user might hear sounds that are somewhat "muddy" or "underwater." Users can have difficulties discerning between male and female voices and detecting the nuances of emotion or sarcasm. What a user hears varies enormously from person to person. One objective measurement, distinguishing notes on a piano, illustrated the variability of the implants' success: In a 2012 study, four out of eleven children with cochlear implants were able to distinguish between a C and a C-sharp. But one child could not tell a C from an F, and two others heard no difference between a C and an E.

The effectiveness of cochlear implants also depends very much on the setting. Using them in noisy places, like a cocktail party, can be challenging. In 2020, a group of Australian researchers published a scientific review, a meta-analysis of research on the effectiveness of implants in adults. The study found that the quality of the sound that patients were able to hear varied considerably, as did their ability to understand speech. After surgery, patients on average understood 74 percent of sentences read to them in a quiet setting and 50 percent in a noisy environment.

Cochlear implants are clearly imperfect. But thousands of profoundly deaf people use them to interact with the hearing world, whether at jobs or socially. As of 2019, around 740,000 cochlear devices had been implanted worldwide, according to the FDA. In the United States, 65,000 children were fitted with the devices, with each operation typically costing in the neighborhood of $30,000 to $50,000.

For the deaf community worldwide, implants have been a point of debate and controversy. In the early days of their adoption many deaf people were wary of them. They feared the devices would buttress the idea that deaf people needed to be "cured" and that technology could do it. Deafness was not cancer, they argued, not something that needed treatment in the same way a deadly disease does. With sign language, members of the community were fully able to communicate with one another. The prospect of "fixing" deaf children raised questions about the future of an entire culture, of Deaf Culture. For more than a century deaf people had battled for the right to sign-language instruction. They worried what would happen to their language, and to the entire way of life that came with it, if children were urged to accept implants. What if Basque speakers or Navajo speakers were told they were better off getting a device implanted in their brain because their language was too obscure?

In the United States, enrollment in deaf schools, the heart of deaf communities across the country, was falling for a variety of reasons, and the deaf community saw implants as hastening their decline.

The technology bitterly divided families over whether parents should have their deaf children implanted, a tension captured in the 2000 documentary film *Sound and Fury,* where a deaf couple, Peter and Nita Artinian, decide against providing a cochlear device for their five-year-old daughter, Heather. At one point in the film, Peter Artinian lashes out, "Hearing people think that deafness is limiting, that we can't succeed. I say, no way!"

Two decades later, the suspicions toward implants have by no means disappeared in the deaf community. But attitudes have softened somewhat. The availability of implants coincided with hard-fought victories for deaf activists in other areas: greater acknowledgment of ASL as a language like any other; the passage of the Americans with Disabilities Act in 1990, which mandated sign-language interpreting for places like hospitals. Technologies like closed-captioned television and the iPhone bridged some of the gap between hearing and deaf communities.

In one measure of the reduced wariness toward implants, five years after *Sound and Fury* was made, Heather, the girl whose parents had vehemently rejected the device, received one, along with her mother and other deaf relatives. "I just wanted to be able to communicate with the majority of people who live in this world who are hearing," Heather told a publication at Harvard Law School, where she graduated in 2018.

In a moving speech at Georgetown University, which Heather attended as an undergraduate, she discussed how difficult it was to learn how to speak. After receiving the implant, she had speech therapy classes every day after school, and at first her classmates did not understand her. She sometimes had to rely on sign-language interpreters. But she continued to refine her speech. "I was willing to put in the work and I saw the results," she said in the George-town talk. "I had a wonderful family who supported me through all this," she said. Some words like "Maryland" and "things" and "human beings" are muffled in her Georgetown speech. For people unfamiliar with her story, it might have been challenging to follow. She spoke about how her roommates asked her to repeat herself "all the time" because they didn't understand her. But Heather, like Dominic Turner, had forged this uncommon path. They didn't have to reside exclusively in the hearing world. Or in the deaf world. They just stay in the "middle," as Heather Artinian called it.

Dominic Turner's early years with the cochlear implant are testament to the hard work of learning to speak. It was a painstaking journey, and one that left him uncertain for years where he fit in. At the same time, it was a wondrous process that hearing people take for granted. Gaining hearing when he was five years old meant that he had to consciously learn the sounds that he was hearing. His grandmother Joanie Jackson, who raised him, would point out sounds throughout the day.

"Listen! That's the sound of water," she would tell Dominic. How else would he know what the trickle of liquid sounded like if it wasn't pointed out to him? "And that's a bird. Did you hear it?"

"It was constantly identifying sounds," Jackson remembered.

For years, this process would require, for Dominic, the concerted study of sound. Even as a teenager, a decade after he received his implant, he found that he needed to concentrate on speech to ascertain it.

"English is a foreign language to me," Dominic said.

Dominic Turner lives in a world that hearing people might find hard to imagine.

He tunes in to the hearing world when he wants to: At the beach, he likes hearing the sounds of waves. He wears his implants to the movies. He enjoys the roar of certain car engines. But he removes his implant and enters a world without hearing when he is around noises that he finds unpleasant. He dislikes high-pitched voices and people who laugh too loudly. He finds the sounds of traffic rushing past distracting, and in those settings he prefers to hear nothing at all.

At school and on the football field, he keeps the implant off and thrives in the world that he is most comfortable in, signing with his friends and teachers.

Dominic is convinced that when he gets married, it will be to a deaf woman.

Communicating with deaf friends is faster and "more effortless."

"I just feel that it's more fun," he said.

12

Fame

The Cubs continued their winning streak through October, and with each victory word spread through Southern California's deaf community that the team was not only undefeated but trouncing their opponents.

In a game against Desert Chapel, a small Christian school in Palm Springs, Coach Adams noticed that the defense was playing very soft, with only two or three Desert Chapel players on the line and the rest positioned deep, as if expecting long passes on every play. Adams adjusted his game plan and handed the ball off to Phillip Castaneda. Again and again, Phillip bounced off defenders like a pinball and raced up the field. He had a monster game, scoring four touchdowns and racking up 232 yards. On defense, he had five tackles.

Phillip had moved from sleeping in the Target parking lot into a room in a nearby house. And his feats on the field impressed everyone—coaches, players, fans.

And his long-suffering mother.

"It filled her broken heart to see me succeed," Phillip said.

At home games, alumni returned to the campus, some of them with walkers and wheelchairs, to watch CSDR beat yet another opponent. The bleachers started to resemble class reunions. Patricia Davis, one of the school's first fifty-six students when it had opened nearly seven decades earlier, beamed from her seat on the sidelines. "This has been a long time coming," she said. Scott Raymer, the former defensive end who had played under Coach Lanzi, came back for a piece of the glory that had eluded his generation. "Finally, we have bragging rights at this school," he said.

The alumni were flanked by the players' nervous parents, who stood on the edge of the field and on the dirt track, a dozen yards from the sidelines. They came with extended families, aunts and uncles, nieces and nephews, many of them also deaf. Felix Gonzales's mother, Delia, who had comforted her son during his days of despair and frustration playing on a hearing team, talked about how being on the Cubs had changed her son's life. The mother of Christian Jimenez, the co-captain and lineman, recalled how her son had also felt lonely and frustrated when he played on a hearing team. Being on the Cubs, she said, "really changed him." He was more confident. And happier.

Another regular at the games, Jeremias Valencia, had an especially tight connection to CSDR. He was both an alumnus—he had broken a school record for career points in basketball in 1999—and the father of Jory Valencia, the Cubs' wide receiver who was having a standout season.

Jeremias was the first generation in his family who learned to read and write, not to mention attend college. Part Mexican and part Apache, the family came from southern Arizona. According to a story passed down in the family for three generations, they had been swindled out of six hundred acres of land north of the Mexican border in the late nineteenth century. Jeremias's great-grandfather was told he would be given $200 if he signed a piece of paper. He didn't realize that it was the deed to his land, which today is filled with golf resorts and casinos.

The family retained their small house outside Tucson, but the neighborhood became gang territory, and the Valencias looked for somewhere to move. When Jeremias was in his early teens, the family piled into a yellow school bus, stenciled "Valencia" on the spot that would normally announce the school district, and made the trek to Riverside. They parked the bus in the parking lot across the street from CSDR, the same piece of pavement where Phillip Castaneda would sleep decades later. Within days, the family found a house to rent, and Jeremias enrolled at the school. The Valencias then began to fill the basketball record books, starting with Jeremias's 1999 season. His son Noah would break a Riverside record, scoring seventy-one points in a single game. And Jory would be selected as the league MVP in basketball his senior year.

On the football field, Jory used his basketball skills as a wide receiver and safety, often outjumping his opponents. His Instagram account was Airvalencia. He would end the season with seventeen receiving touchdowns and thirteen interceptions.

I met Jory and his father in the second week of November 2021. The Cubs, now 10-0, were playing Desert Christian, a team from just outside Edwards Air Force Base, where Charles Yeager had broken the sound barrier and the space shuttle had made its first landing.

I had sold my editor at *The New York Times* on a story about this obscure Southern California football team after seeing the email from Tony Thurmond, the head of the California Department of Education. I had broken away from my coverage of Northern California and hopped into my car bound for Riverside. Now I stood on the sidelines as the game was about to begin. Jeremias Valencia, standing nearby, was basking in the Cubs' success. "All the hard work has finally paid off," he said.

I was accustomed to attending my son's football games at our local public high school east of San Francisco, and the scene at CSDR had a very different vibe from the Friday night lights of my son's team. There was no national anthem, no loudspeaker to announce the plays, no music during pauses in the game. Children ran to the concession stand and signed their orders. The Cubs' sidelines and the bleachers were a whir of signed conversations. On the CSDR campus, visitors who did not know ASL were the outsiders, or, to use another word, were handicapped by their lack of sign language. Like monolingual American tourists in Tokyo, it was on them to find a way to make themselves understood.

The Cubs were undefeated, but the field where they played had the neglected feel of an underdog. You had to squint to read the red numbers on the decades-old scoreboard. The bleachers looked as if they had been salvaged from a junkyard, and the field was illuminated by a series of diesel generators that you might see lighting up a construction site. The end zones were beyond the reach of the lights, and one got the impression that scoring a touchdown meant disappearing into darkness. Coach Adams liked to point out that when administrators at CSDR gave tours of the school, they often skipped showing the football field.

Watching the game was by no means a silent experience. There was the loud drone of the generators, the passing freight trains, and the clamor of football noises coming from the field: the collisions of pads and helmets, the referees' whistles. But play proceeded in a more visual dimension than at my son's games, as if parts of the soundtrack had been deleted.

The Cubs won the game 84–12. Another rout. The victory would send them to the semifinals of the Southern California playoffs. CSDR was two games away from playing in a championship game for the first time in school history. As a small school—there were only 128 students enrolled in the high school—winning the championship would place them as the top eight-man team in the small-school division in Southern California. It wasn't national glory, but no team at the school had come close to achieving it.

In the article that I wrote about the team, I quoted Aaron Williams, the head coach of Desert Christian, the hearing team the

Cubs had just defeated. He had a warning for future opponents of the Cubs.

"I would say be careful in thinking that you have an advantage," Williams said. "They communicate better than any team I have ever coached against."

The article, published in *The New York Times* on the Monday after the game, went viral.

Calls from television stations and newspapers flooded the school's switchboard. Erika Thompson, the school's communications director, received sixty-six requests from media outlets and documentary filmmakers in the days after the article ran. All wanted to come to the school to interview the coaches and players. Some television stations reached out multiple times. "Weren't you just here yesterday?" Thompson would reply to an inquiring news station. No, that was the afternoon news program, they would reply; we're the evening broadcast. *Good Morning America* came to profile the team. So did *The Today Show.* There were requests from Spanish-language broadcasters and an Australian television network.

"Deaf High School Football Team's Remarkable Comeback Inspires America" was the headline on the NBC News website. ABC News named the team the "Persons of the Week."

The TV correspondents competed for corniest scripts with deaf puns. "With an 11-0 record, the Cubs are one win away from their division varsity championship game," said one reporter. "That's impressive enough. But then you realize none of them are talking to each other—at least not with words!" Another correspondent chimed in: "No hut-hut-hike for these players!"

Disney contacted the school and began negotiating to film a series on the team. Separately, Keith Adams received offers for the life rights of his story. Producers reached out to me and *The New York Times,* asking about movie rights. The National Football League contacted the school and asked that the team's captains take part in the coin toss at the Super Bowl, which was being held in Inglewood, outside Los Angeles, that year. Coach Adams, who accompanied the players to the big game, met a representative from Nike who offered to outfit the team for the next season for free.

Adams was also invited to attend the Pro Bowl in Las Vegas and was nominated coach of the year by the Los Angeles Rams. He went to the draft as a guest of the NFL.

All this attention wore down some of the players, especially Trevin Adams, who was shy to begin with. The contrast was striking: In television interviews he was demure, polite, and reserved. In games, he was back to being the smash-your-opponent Trevin. When *The Kelly Clarkson Show* invited Coach Adams, Trevin, and Christian Jimenez to talk about their season, Trevin initially balked. He had smiled for enough cameras already. His father had to persuade him.

"You know what, Trevin, this puts us on the map," Keith told his son. "And it puts deaf people on the map. There are a lot of people out there who are ignorant about who we are and what we do. This spotlight that we are getting is so temporary. And not many people have this opportunity."

Trevin dutifully sat on the stage, politely answered questions in his red Cubs jersey. At the end of the segment, Clarkson announced that the show would donate $25,000 to a fund for a new stadium.

Jesse Aguilar, the coach of Noli Indian, was watching television and saw the coach and players who had beat him the first game of the season. He snapped a picture of the screen and showed it to his players. "This has to be us someday," he told his Native American players.

The attention that the Cubs received did not stop there. It translated to real dollars for the school. The administration of California's governor, Gavin Newsom, announced plans for a $43 million new sports complex and stadium that would replace not just the football field but the facilities for track, softball, baseball, and soccer.

It was a cascade of national news stories on a scale that the school had never seen before. For the team, now the pressure was really on. They had captured the nation's imagination. They had burrowed their way into the hearts of mothers, of teachers, of anyone who saw their story as an allegory for overcoming adversity.

The California School for the Deaf, Riverside basked in the publicity and saw it as an opportunity for outreach and education. Reporters, and by extension the public, were asking about deafness, about American Sign Language, about whether deafness could provide an edge on the playing field. And all this was being discussed on segments showing game footage of Cubs players streaking down the field toward the end zone.

13

The Deaf Brain

Dr. Eddie Chang, a neurosurgeon in San Francisco, stood in the operating theater holding a surgical saw that he would use to cut away a piece of skull the size of an iPhone. The goal of the operation was to remove a patient's brain tumor. Dr. Chang had been referred the case of this middle-aged California man because the tumor in question was near a part of the brain associated with language. This very delicate procedure, known as an awake craniotomy, was Dr. Chang's specialty. The patient's head is secured in a type of vise to keep it perfectly still. Then, after the piece of skull is cut away, the patient is awakened from general anesthesia and asked to count or read a text on a computer screen. The surgeon uses a probe and delivers small doses of electrical current to explore the part of the brain associated with language. The idea is that the patient continues speaking while the surgeon maps out the crucial parts of the brain. If the patient stops counting, the surgeon knows to leave that area intact. For this particular operation, which took place on a rainy November day in 2012, there was a twist. The patient was profoundly deaf. Instead of using his voice, he would sign. Dr. Chang, who had never performed the operation on a deaf person before, needed to map out a deaf brain.

Until the mid-nineteenth century, surgeons had only vague ideas of where language was processed in the brain. But on a spring day in 1861, in a hospital just south of Paris, a brilliant and inquisitive French surgeon in his late thirties, Pierre Paul Broca, made a major discovery. Paris at that time was arguably the center of global medical advances, and Broca had been engaged in a debate with his colleagues about where language was generated. On that spring day, he set out to examine the brain of a recently deceased patient. The patient provided potential insights because two decades before his death he had lost the ability to speak. Broca hoped he could find in the autopsy the damaged parts of the brain and map out its importance to language.

Born in Sainte-Foy-la-Grande, one of a string of well-preserved medieval towns east of Bordeaux, Broca was raised in a well-educated Protestant household, his father having served as a surgeon in Napoleon's army. His home was five miles upriver from the Château de Montaigne, birthplace of the Renaissance philosopher Michel de Montaigne, who three centuries earlier had famously asked, "Que sais-je?"—"What do I know?" In his medical studies, Broca seemed to be infused with that spirit of skepticism and with an adherence to observation, to trial and error. That Broca was from a Protestant family was important because it unshackled him from the tenets and dogma of the Roman Catholic Church, which at the time was in a pitched battle with the precepts of Darwinism. Broca, who would repeatedly clash with the ecclesiastical authorities during the course of his career, would write in his memoir, "I would rather be a transformed ape than a degenerate son of Adam."

The brain that Broca would gently poke and prod in 1861 belonged to a man named Leborgne, fifty-one years old at his death. Leborgne had been given the nickname Tan—pronounced like the word for "time" in French, *temps,* because it was the only sound Leborgne could make. In his detailed description of the case, Broca noted that Tan had been alert and intelligent. "He understood everything that you said to him," Broca wrote in the *Bulletins de la Société Anatomique de Paris,* the journal of the Anatomical Society of Paris. "He actually had a very refined ear. But whatever the question that you asked him, he always responded 'tan, tan.'"

In his examination of Tan's brain, Broca traced a large lesion to a part of the frontal lobe in the left hemisphere, an area situated a few inches above the left ear.

Broca hypothesized, and future analysis of other patients would confirm, that the area was crucial to controlling speech. The damage to this area explained why Leborgne could produce only the sound "tan," again and again. Today, that part of the brain is known to neurosurgeons as Broca's area.

A little more than a decade after Broca's discovery, a German neurologist, Carl Wernicke, would document a part of the brain that governs language comprehension as well as the ability to string words together.

In the century and a half since these discoveries, generations of neurosurgeons have relied on that early mapping of the brain, Broca's area and Wernicke's area, in their treatment of stroke patients and others with brain injuries that cause aphasia, the difficulty or inability to speak and write.

At the operating table in 2012, Eddie Chang knew that his patient's tumor had started to affect his ability to sign. He wanted to be as aggressive as possible in removing the tumor but needed to avoid cutting the part of the brain that controlled sign language. The patient, now awake and signing, lay on his side as Dr. Chang stood on the other side of a surgical curtain staring into the exposed brain, not knowing what to expect. As he began the mapping process—every person's brain is organized slightly differently—he moved his electrical probe toward Broca's area. Dr. Chang touched the brain's surface with his probe, and the device delivered the electrical current. At that moment, the patient stopped signing. He repeated the exercise, asking the patient to resume signing and delivering the electrical current. Again, the patient stopped signing.

Eddie Chang successfully removed the tumor. But he had trouble sleeping that night. His training had told him that Broca's area controlled speech, which occurs with the complex coordination of more than a hundred muscles in the mouth and throat. But what he had witnessed, and what brain imaging studies had suggested in the decades before Chang's surgery, was that this part of the brain was associated with something bigger than just speech. It was a sort of communication center. "We have a wiring for language, and it doesn't matter if it's spoken or gestural," Dr. Chang said.

Five years later, Dr. Chang's understanding of this part of the brain broadened even further when he performed a similar operation on a musician who stopped playing guitar when the electrical current was applied to Broca's area.

Humans are constantly moving their hands: a quarterback throwing a pass, a person pointing to the cut of beef he wants at the meat counter, a woman waving goodbye. But although they might use the same muscles as someone communicating with sign language, the movements are processed differently in the brain.

.   .   .

For centuries the prevailing view of sign language was that it was a primitive way of communicating. This was a stigma that was ironically reinforced in the nineteenth century by the scientific revolution that came with Darwinism.

The publishing of Darwin's *On the Origin of Species* in 1859 brought with it popular theories that sign languages were "low in the scale of evolutionary progress," according to the American Sign Language historian Douglas Baynton. This lowly notion of signing was a great departure from the Parisian admiration of sign language just decades earlier, when visitors to the school founded by Charles-Michel de l'Epée admired sign language as being "natural" and thus perhaps closer to God.

With Darwinism came the notion that signing was a rudimentary communication system closer to ape than man. In the lingo of the time, sign languages were the domain of the "savage." It was in this context that educators decided to ban sign languages at the 1880 Milan conference.

This prevailing skepticism of sign language among educators did not begin to change until the 1960s, when a scholar of classic English literature and a specialist in Chaucer, William Stokoe, began a career-long campaign to prove to the world that sign languages were like any oral languages. He published a series of works on the structure and linguistic principles of American Sign Language. He dissected ASL and showed its syntax and grammar. He co-wrote the first ASL dictionary that, in addition to explaining the meanings and usage of signs, gave a linguistic analysis of the parts of each sign. He dissected the language and categorized it into phonemes, as one would do with a spoken language. In one respect ASL was very much like an oral language: fluent signers could detect accents, the signing equivalent of a southern drawl.

Further studies carried out by David Corina, Karen Emmorey, and many other scientists would trace the neural pathways of sign language using brain imaging. The research would confirm that the mind processed sign language in a way similar to how it processed spoken languages. When the patient in Dr. Chang's operating room used his hands for sign language, his brain deployed language pathways. When he was just moving his hands around without any intention to communicate, the brain signals moved along a different pathway.

Other studies led by Laura-Ann Petitto, a cognitive neuroscientist, showed how deaf and hearing children acquired languages in the same ways, along the same neural pathways and in the same time frame. Petitto showed that just as hearing babies vocally babble at around six months, deaf, signing babies babble with their hands, moving them rhythmically and with sign-language syllabic structures. In other words, while hearing babies made sounds like "ba ba ba," deaf babies moved their hands in ways distinct from their hearing counterparts, in movements that the researchers judged were the equivalent of sign-language babble.

The evidence that scientists accumulated about sign language rendered what Petitto described as a "most remarkable revolution in thinking in our modern world regarding what human language is and what makes up being human."

"Speech and language have now been biologically decoupled," she wrote in the 2014 book *Deaf Gain*. "Speech is not language. 'Language' resides in our brains and is distinct from its production."

Today, American Sign Language is recognized in the field of linguistics as the equivalent of any other complex and natural human language. It is also, in the words of Thomas Holcomb, a deaf scholar, "the central component" of the deaf identity.

14

Avalon

Under hazy blue skies, the Cubs' coaching staff led twenty-one players wearing white jerseys onto the *Starship Express*. The white jerseys with red lettering were reserved for away games, and by the standards of high school football this particular journey was pushing the concept of "away" to its limits. The *Starship Express* was a ferry that would take the team to Santa Catalina Island for the semifinal game of the Southern California championship. Leaving from Long Beach, the thirty-mile journey into the waters of the Pacific was scheduled to take about an hour. As the boat zigzagged its way through the giant harbor and gained speed, the steady roar of the engines and the brisk breezes coming off the ocean were enough to make conversations for hearing passengers nearly impossible. But it made no difference to the Cubs who stood on the deck of the ferry, their hair and jerseys whipped by the wind as they excitedly signed to one another. Alexandero Morales, a CSDR employee who doubled as the Cubs' game statistician, turned to a hearing reporter standing next to him. "Don't you wish you were deaf?" he signed.

On the same ferry were news crews from three different television networks, some carrying the transmitters that they would use to send their footage. To the Cubs, it felt as if the world were now watching them closely. "We're excited to prove that we are a good team," Bryan Smith, a sophomore cornerback, signed from the aft deck of the ferry.

But media fatigue had already started to set in. The daily interviews that featured reporters asking the same questions had been a distraction. "It's hard to concentrate with so many reporters and cameras around," said Ryan Zarembka, a Cubs assistant coach who knew the boys especially well. He had been head coach of the middle school team that had gone undefeated three years earlier.

. . .

Santa Catalina Island is known in Southern California as a place for weekend getaways, for scuba diving and hiking, for palm trees and beaches. But the island is also home to a tight-knit community in Avalon, the main town, that has worked and lived there for multiple generations. Many are descendants of the laborers brought from California and Mexico by William Wrigley Jr., the Chicago chewing gum magnate who bought up most of Santa Catalina in 1919.

Among the offspring of the laborers was Nick Morones, a graduate of Avalon High School who had played quarterback on the school's football team and had returned after college as a physical education teacher and head coach of the Avalon Lancers. In this, his first year, he had led the team to the semifinals with a 7-2 record. And now on a Friday in mid-November 2021, he awaited the arrival of the players and coaches of the California School for the Deaf, Riverside. Morones liked to think that Avalon has a unique home-field advantage. Opposing teams are either exhausted by the journey, seasick from the ferry crossing, or so enchanted by the island that they have forgotten about football.

This was partly true for the Cubs, who had driven more than two hours just to get to the ferry terminal and were now slicing through the swells of the Pacific. Jory Valencia had picked up a bad case of food poisoning two days earlier that had left him tired and weakened. He was rallying, standing on the rear deck with his teammates, but looking wan.

Like the Cubs, the Avalon Lancers were known as a very physical team. Morones attributed this to the fact that many of his players had been hardened by years working part-time jobs in construction and tourism and all the other tasks needed to keep the tourist town running. Their days started early at school and finished late at their workplaces. Growing up on an island, they were also born swimmers, something that contributed to their athleticism, Morones reasoned.

The game against the Cubs was highly anticipated in Avalon. Many people had caught glimpses of the news coverage of what all the broadcasts described as a remarkable deaf team. Now Avalon residents saw the TV crews and the Cubs players wandering the streets like some invading army. "They're on our turf and it's time to take them down," Morones told his players. He expected an old-fashioned, smashmouth game like "gladiators going to battle." He would be proved correct.

The small stadium where the Lancers play is carved into the rounded hills above Avalon and ringed by palm and eucalyptus trees. It's an idyllic spot for a football game, and Avalon's aqua-blue-and-yellow uniforms seemed a perfect reflection of Santa Catalina's azure waters and the sunshine that blessed the place.

Dozens of Cubs supporters and families had made the long trek to Avalon, and they sat in the bleachers perched on a hillside above the field. Felix Gonzales's mother wore a T-shirt she made for the occasion. It was bright red, with a picture of Felix playing football. In bold yellow letters it read, "Felix Gonzales. That's my son."

Students at CSDR had hand-painted large posters that the Cubs' entourage had taped to the chain-link fence along the visitors' sideline. WE BELIEVE IN YOU, read one of the larger signs.

But the Cubs' fans were outnumbered by supporters of the home team. There are relatively few cars on the island, so they drove their golf carts to the stadium and watched from a ridge overlooking the field. A group of Avalon teenagers stood in the tall grass behind the end zone. Residents of the island spend their days surrounded by tourists, but at the Lancers' football games they could come together as neighbors. "One team, one community, one heart," Morones liked to say.

At dusk, as the teams warmed up on the field, the loudspeaker blared "Bad Moon Rising" by Creedence Clearwater Revival.

I see the bad moon arising
I see trouble on the way

When the national anthem began playing, echoing through the canyons of the island, Ken Watson, the Cubs' assistant coach, had to remind the players to remove their helmets.

The Cubs won the toss and elected to receive.

On the first play of the game, as the Avalon cheerleaders chanted, "Defense! Defense!" Trevin dropped back and was immediately swarmed by four Avalon defenders and slung down violently. The play never had a chance.

The Cubs then tried a screen pass. But Trevin, scrambling for his life, couldn't get off a good throw. The ball flew past the outstretched hands of Enos Zornoza and hit the artificial turf.

Phillip Castaneda then went in motion on the next play and got a handoff from Trevin. He sprinted toward the perimeter, but a stocky Avalon linebacker easily read the play and, towering over Phillip, brought him to the ground.

After three downs, the Cubs had gained a single yard and were forced to punt. Avalon's speed, their twitchy aggressiveness, and their sheer physicality were on display.

"Thataway, Avalon!" yelled a Lancers supporter from the stands. "It's not going to be close!"

Avalon had a decidedly more impressive start in their first drive, including two runs for fifteen yards each. But the drive stalled with a holding penalty. The Lancers were forced to try a field goal. The kick was so powerful it went through the uprights, over the chain-link fence, and into the palm trees. Avalon was on the board first, but with a three-point lead it was the slimmest of margins.

The Cubs' second drive started very badly, with Trevin sacked at his own ten-yard line. But a dump pass to Phillip, who turned on the jets and ran for twenty yards, dug the Cubs out of their hole. A few runs later and Felix Gonzales sealed off the drive with a catch in the end zone.

Kaveh Angoorani stiffened the Cubs' defense and on the next drive forced Avalon to punt. On the snap, Trevin surged through the line, blocked the punt, and found himself in the end zone with the ball. It was odd how quickly the momentum of the game had turned. With the two-point conversion the Cubs were suddenly up 16–3.

The frustration of the initial missteps in the game had fired up the Cubs. They had panicked at their inept start and were now playing with so much passion that one of the referees made an unusual comment to Mark Bayarsky, the interpreter for CSDR who served as the interface between the team and anyone who needed to talk to them.

"Tell the defense to settle down," the ref said.

"Why?" Mark asked.

"So that no one gets hurt."

Avalon began to defeat itself.

A long run was called back by a holding penalty. On the first play of the second quarter, an Avalon receiver fumbled the ball and the Cubs recovered it. The Cubs' subsequent drive resulted in another CSDR touchdown.

The self-destruction then picked up speed: a bad snap resulted in yet another turnover and another Cubs score. The Avalon quarterback threw an interception, and then another. And on Avalon's last drive of the second half, Jory Valencia picked off an Avalon pass for the third time. The Lancers had turned the ball over a stunning five times in two quarters. Avalon fans were in disbelief.

"Come on, Lancers! Get your heads together," someone yelled. At the half, the Cubs were ahead, 48–3.

Even by the high-scoring standards of eight-man ball, the game seemed over. But Coach Morones told his players to fight. If they lost, this would be the last high school game for some of the Avalon players. Morones told them to give it their all. "Look at the stands," he remembers telling his players. "No one has left. The next half, you're just playing for the guys in the stands."

Avalon looked like a different team in the third quarter. The jinx that had flummoxed them in the first half had been blown off the island. On their second play of the half, an Avalon running back mowed down Cubs defenders and ran fifty yards to the end zone. The Avalon quarterback seemed to find superhuman strength, shedding tackle after tackle. Their linemen blocked with heart, plowing Cubs defenders out of their path. When the Cubs were on offense, Avalon swarmed after the ball, denying any meaningful progress on the ground. This was the gladiator football that Coach Morones had predicted. On a Cubs fourth down, they sacked Trevin, smacking him to the ground and then scoring two plays later. In all, they put a remarkable thirty-two points on the board in the third quarter.

The Cubs managed only six points in that quarter, although it was one of the most beautiful plays of the season. Trevin threw a deep ball to Felix, who leaped like an Olympian, grabbed the ball with one hand, and brought it to his chest. Felix is left-handed, but he had caught the ball and tucked it away entirely with his right hand. It was his second acrobatic catch of the game.

By the fourth quarter, the game was making Keith Adams very nervous. The temperature had dipped to the low fifties, but he was still wearing his light polo shirt and shorts. He was generating enough heat pacing the sidelines and exhorting his players to meet the physicality of their opponents.

Avalon scored another sixteen points in the fourth quarter, but it wasn't enough. If football were a game of five quarters, maybe they would have caught up. But they ran out of time. With forty-three seconds on the clock, an onside kick was recovered by Christian Jimenez. The final score was 62–51.

The Avalon players were emotional as they lined up at midfield to shake hands. Some were loudly cursing, clearly devastated by their elimination from the playoffs. But Esteban Chavolla, a stocky defensive end and co-captain of the Lancers, showed grace. With tears rolling down his cheeks, he praised his victorious opponents. "Your team is amazing," he told the Cubs players. "You guys are amazing! Don't let anyone ever tell you you're not. You have everything against you. And you can still do this."

After the game, a television station interviewed Felix Gonzales on the field. He had scored three touchdowns, including the one-handed grab and a diving catch in the end zone. He would later say the game against Avalon was his favorite of his high school career.

"I'm just proud," Felix signed to the television reporter as his mother, a few feet away, watched. "I'm proud to be deaf."

15

Battered

The Cubs had earned their place in the championship game of the California Interscholastic Federation, Southern Section, the largest division in the state. It would mark the first time in California history that a deaf football team competed in the finals in any division.

For Trevin Adams, there had been little time to celebrate after the game in Avalon. He and his family had rushed through the streets to the harbor, where the last ferry to the mainland would soon depart. The adrenaline from the game was still surging through his battered body. But as he settled into his seat in the ferry, he found himself in terrible pain. Getting up to disembark at Long Beach, he had trouble walking down the gangplank onto the pier. He gave his duffel bag to his mother to carry.

The Avalon game had been by far the most physical of the season. It had also been the team's first on an artificial surface that year, and many of the players came away with turf burns. The game took its toll on the team like none before. Felix had exacerbated a hip injury with his diving end-zone catch, and at the same time had scraped the skin off his hip, a wound that would soon become infected. Jory was still recovering from his stomach bug.

And most worrying of all, Trevin was so beat up that for three days he shuffled around his house, delicately planting one foot in front of the other and feeling each step. The Cubs had made it to the championship game, and they had seven days to prepare. But they were battered.

They were also heading off in different directions. There was no school the entire next week for Thanksgiving break, and students had gone home to their families. It was a week that would center on family and recovery, not football. The championship game was scheduled for Saturday, the end of the holiday week and just two days after Thanksgiving.

The coaches had abandoned the notion of holding any on-field practices that week. Keith Adams and Kaveh Angoorani met to strategize. They learned that their opponent in the championship would be Faith Baptist, a powerhouse in eight-man football. Faith Baptist had played in the championship game nineteen times over the last four decades, and had won nine. Keith and Kaveh, new-comers to the big game, watched film and sketched out Faith Baptist's playbook. The two men had been coaching together for years, but this game was on another level entirely, and they had only a few days to prepare.

They were in many ways an unlikely pair: Keith was the Scotch-Irish son of migrants from Oklahoma who settled into a middle-class life in Stockton. Kaveh was born in Iran a decade and a half before Islamic fundamentalists took control of the country. After attending the nation's oldest deaf school in Hartford, Kaveh had made his way in America working at a fast-food restaurant, painting county jails, and ultimately doing one of the most American things an immigrant could do: coaching football.

His bond with Keith was deafness and football. And it was a tight bond. During his second stint as coach, Keith had begged Kaveh to return as defensive coordinator. Kaveh had reluctantly agreed. But Kaveh made it clear that 2021 would be his last season with the Cubs. He was nearing sixty and was eager to wrap up his long career as a deaf educator. After his unlikely path from the streets of Tehran of his youth to his American life in Riverside, California, Kaveh was ready to retire.

16

A Football? But It's Not Round

The shrine of Imam Reza is one of the most sacred sites in Iran, a collection of turquoise minarets, sprawling courtyards, and countless elaborate mosaics that bring millions of visitors to Mashhad, Iran's second-largest city. More people visit the shrine every year than do Mecca in Saudi Arabia.

For Aghdas Kavandi, the shrine was a place to pray for her son, Kaveh, who had been born profoundly deaf. Kaveh was six months old when his grandmother noticed that the boy did not respond to clapping and other sharp or loud noises.

Aghdas had blamed herself for her son's deafness, believing that a fall down a set of stairs during pregnancy had damaged Kaveh in the womb. It was a belief that family members would later disavow after discovering a gene associated with deafness in the family. Regardless, Aghdas spent Kaveh's earliest years fretting about her son, worried that he would have a very difficult life, that he might not be able to support himself, that he would remain single and friendless. Her pilgrimage to the shrine of Imam Reza was a well-trodden one for Shiite Muslims: like Roman Catholics journeying to the spring water in the grotto at Lourdes, Shiite devotees came to pray for healing at the shrine. Aghdas followed a ritual used to pray for the sick, tying a piece of cloth to a gilded gate and spending a night in prayer.

She had reason to be worried about Kaveh, who was born in 1963 in Tehran. Iran was a tough place for a deaf child. Exuberant and jolly as a young boy, Kaveh was well liked by his neighbors and extended family. But farther from the house he was shooed away by adults when they realized he could not hear. Instances of rejection are still sharp in Kaveh's mind decades later. He remembers not being able to buy an ice cream cone because the shop attendant did not have the patience to follow the boy's gestures.

"I was constantly treated like I was just an idiot," Kaveh said.

Kaveh's parents had enrolled him in a deaf school in Tehran, a place of rigid discipline, where the teachers sometimes used corporal punishment, common at the time in Tehran, according to Kaveh's sister, Laleh, who is two years older. At the school Kaveh learned a system of gestures that allowed him to communicate with teachers and fellow students. It was not a full sign language but a method, based on the Farsi language, to complement lip-reading; the gestures were used to denote sounds that could not easily be ascertained from the lips, a method called cued speech.

Kaveh struggled in school and was not very good at reading lips. In fifth grade he managed to pass a national exam, a key milestone in the Iranian education system, but he wondered if that was because his mother had bribed someone in officialdom.

Where he excelled was on the streets around his neighborhood in Tehran, playing soccer with the boys of his block. The Iran of the 1960s and 1970s was nothing like the strict Islamic theocracy that came to power in 1979. Women were not obliged to cover their heads; there wasn't the strict segregation between the sexes that would come with the Islamic revolution. And Tehran was a cosmopolitan city, filled with Europeans and Americans, both as tourists and as expatriates.

Kaveh became friends with two German boys who lived one block over and who showed off some impressive soccer tricks, flicking the ball from behind their heels over their heads. They showed Kaveh the art of the blind pass.

Sports served as his connection with the German brothers and the other hearing boys of the neighborhood. A natural athlete, Kaveh learned to kick a soccer ball with just the right spin so that it would arc into the goal, a move that would be popularized as "bending it like Beckham," for the English footballer.

He was a good goalie, too, something he attributes in part to his deafness. He felt it gave him an ability to concentrate on the ball that his hearing friends, distracted by the antics of their teammates, did not share.

Kaveh's athleticism, and his hours of practice, paid off when his friends would come to the door, soccer ball in hand, and ask for him.

"I had to work harder and prove myself," he remembered. "I had to show them that I was just as good as, or better than, them. They needed me because I was a good player."

Despite his successes on the playing field, and the happiness that it brought him, his mother remained deeply concerned. She took him on his first overseas trip, to France, ostensibly to visit relatives, but while in Paris they visited the offices of a doctor who examined him. After the consultation, she was distraught, and Kaveh would later learn that the doctor had determined that no operation could cure his deafness.

His mother soon worked out another plan: an American woman had told her about the American School for the Deaf in Connecticut. Aghdas would send her son to the United States.

Kaveh's father was dead set against the idea.

"You don't send a deaf child to America," Kaveh remembers him saying. "Who's going to take care of him?"

They argued for months, but Kaveh's mother stuck to her plan. She teamed up with another family of a deaf child, Siamak, and proposed that the two boys travel together to America.

A death in the family—Kaveh's maternal grandfather—plunged the family into mourning. But it also made the plan to send Kaveh to America more viable. His grandparents had been living on the second floor of their house in Tehran, and now the family was able to put the space up for rent. Kaveh's grandmother moved in with him and his family, and an American couple moved into the grandparents' old place. The rent that they paid was enough to send Kaveh abroad.

The Americans renting the apartment had a teenage son named Kenny, and despite their age difference—Kaveh was eleven at the time—the two became friends. Kenny showed Kaveh and his friends a ball he had brought from America.

Kaveh recalled the moment.

"He showed me this thing, and he said it was a football. I said, 'Football?' But it's not round. He said, 'Hold on, let me show you. Come outside.' We were making fun of him, trying to kick the ball. But he said, 'No, no, no. You throw it. You catch it.' He got frustrated with us. We tried throwing it. People were getting hit in the forehead. We struggled. We just thought it was funny."

Over the next two years, Kaveh would catch snippets of American football games on television. There were three television channels in Iran at the time, and one of them would show American programs.

Kaveh understood almost nothing of the game but admired the uniforms of the Dallas Cowboys, the bold blue stars on their helmets. Decades later in California, he would remain a devoted Cowboys fan. With his friends in Tehran, Kaveh stayed committed to soccer. They had no time for the odd-shaped ball and the confusing game.

In 1976, he would leave for the United States with his classmate Siamak. They flew into John F. Kennedy airport and then transferred to a small plane for the short hop to Hartford. Their first meal was at McDonald's.

The American School for the Deaf was terrifying for the two boys. The blizzard of sign language, the way the students so effortlessly signed back and forth. Kaveh had learned some basic American Sign Language from an American expatriate in Tehran. But it would take months before he would be comfortable signing with his new classmates.

He once again found comfort in sports. He inquired about a soccer team but was told that there was none. Why not try football, they urged him. Kaveh quickly took to the sport. He played both sides of the ball, becoming a linebacker and a fullback. He was fast and above-average size. He excelled.

"Once I started to play, I absolutely fell in love with the sport," Kaveh said. "The physicality of it. The hits. The strategy of it. And of course it's American. I wanted to be like one of them. I wanted to be an American."

He marveled at how seriously Americans took high school sports. In Tehran he was used to playing for fun with his friends. There was no system of organized scholastic sports teams playing one another in Iran. He embraced the competitiveness. It was a love affair with a game that would endure throughout his decades in the United States.

But first he would have to make a living. When he graduated from the Hartford school, he flew to California to live with his cousin Mehran Mohamadi, who had grown up a few blocks away in Tehran and had immigrated to the United States as a university student just before the 1979 Iranian revolution.

Mehran remembers picking up Kaveh at the airport in Los Angeles and marveling at what an "all-American boy" he had become. The jeans, the haircut, the striped rugby shirts. One of the first things they did was go to an ice cream shop, where Kaveh ordered a huge banana split.

Kaveh found work at Burger King, at the grill, then painting for a Los Angeles–area municipality, including the local jail, then in a one-hour photo shop.

When the manager at the photo shop told him to stay in the back room and not interface with customers because of his deafness, Kaveh showed a further sign he had adapted well to his adopted country: he hired a lawyer and threatened to sue. The shop settled the case for $25,000, and Kaveh used the money to go to college. When his mother in Iran learned that her deaf son had won a lawsuit in America and had received such a large windfall, she was intrigued. "Sue more people!" she said.

Life in America had its quirks: Once while Kaveh was talking to a deaf friend in Los Angeles, a man pulled up a chair and watched intently as they signed to each other. Kaveh, always a burly presence, stood up and motioned for the gawker to scram.

A few years later he was having dinner with his deaf girlfriend and soon-to-be wife, Mary Torres, at In-N-Out Burger, the iconic California burger joint. The couple saw a drunken man sitting nearby who had the look of a gang member. The man became aggressive. When he flashed a handgun in his waistband, Kaveh and Mary bolted.

They had reason to be fearful. An Associated Press story from the time reported on a nineteen-year-old deaf woman killed in her car in Los Angeles when gang members fired on her because they mistook her ASL conversation to be signs of a rival gang. "It's not uncommon as a prelude to shooting for gang members to exchange hand signs, indicating what gang they're in," the AP quoted Detective Dan Andrews saying.

After he earned a degree from Gallaudet University, Kaveh's life drifted back to football. He took a job at the California School for the Deaf in Riverside in 2002 and met Keith Adams, who was looking for help coaching the team.

The job at the school allowed him to buy a brand-new three-bedroom home in Riverside with a small swimming pool in the back. By California standards it was reasonable: $228,500.

For his mother, who visited him in California, it was a huge achievement. She saw her son's two-story home, his cars, and the swimming pool; Kaveh was the first person in the family ever to have a pool at home.

"She was very impressed with that. In her way of thinking, it was, 'Wow, he has so much even though he's deaf.' She's proud. She's proud because people thought she was crazy sending me to America, and look at the end result."

Aghdas—who traveled to the shrine of Imam Reza to beg for her son's well-being, who had fought to send him to the other side of the world for his schooling, and who had fretted endlessly about what future a deaf boy might have—could now be at peace.

"In some ways she thinks her prayers might have worked," Kaveh said.

17

Underdog Meets Top Dog

When word got out that the Cubs had made it to the championship game, demand for tickets surged. Hundreds of people from across the deaf community in Southern California made it known they wanted to attend. The championship would be played as a home game for the Cubs because their semifinal, at Avalon, had been an away game for them. But the worn-out bleachers at the home football field could host only a hundred people. Other spectators would be able to stand on the track and on the fringes of the field. But the CSDR administrators realized that they could accommodate only a fraction of the fans who wanted to witness the first football championship in California to feature a deaf team. They had to move the game.

They settled on John W. North High School, three miles away, a Riverside public school with a stadium that could seat thousands.

The change in venue made little difference to the Cubs' opponents, Faith Baptist. They would still have to drive two hours from their campus in Canoga Park, a neighborhood in the San Fernando Valley northwest of downtown Los Angeles.

The championship game would feature two schools with very strong identities: CSDR's students rallied around their deafness.

And Faith Baptist, founded in 1963 by a pastor as part of an evangelical ministry, had a strong conservative Christian ethic that was infused into the school's curriculum and campus life.

The school's mission statement declared that it sought to "train the student in the way of life presented in the Scriptures while giving him a good general education."

Faith Baptist students have half an hour of Bible study three times a week and chapel the other two days. They are banned on campus from using curse words or listening to music that has explicit lyrics. The boys are required to keep their faces shaved and their hair short. The football team says a prayer before and after every practice and game. And the cheerleaders wear uniforms that by California standards seem a throwback to a previous era, skirts flowing below the knee. Faith infuses the school—and the football program.

With an annual tuition set at less than $8,000, the school is on the affordable side in the Los Angeles area and attracts a mix of middle- to upper-income families: teachers, doctors, blue-collar workers. The student body is white, Latino, and Asian, including a sizable number of students of Filipino background.

"It's a strict school," said Rob Davidson, who shared the job of head coach with the school founder's son, Jon Rasmussen. "It teaches kids rules and morals and behaving."

Davidson, who had coached the team since 2006, was its main strategist. He was born in the Bronx, grew up on Long Island, studied in England, and at one point lived in the Boston area. His accent seemed to carry a morsel of each of those places. He divided his time between coaching kids the finer points of football and touring the world as the chief executive of a pharmaceutical company that specializes in delivering medicine to developing countries. He was proud that despite his peripatetic schedule he would make it back from his overseas business trips to preside over practices. "When you commit, you commit," he said. "I can operate on very little sleep."

No one could complain if Coach Davidson missed a practice here and there: the last time the Faith Baptist Contenders had posted a losing record was a decade earlier. The championship game would be top dog versus underdog. Faith Baptist's winning record was a mirror image of the Cubs' losing streak.

Faith Baptist was 10-2 coming into the championship game and had a large roster, thirty-four players, swelling with talent. In the playoffs, they had demolished their opponents, outscoring them 176–6.

Faith Baptist also had some heft: One of their tight ends was six feet, eight inches and 250 pounds, towering over his opponents on the field. The center, also 250 pounds but much shorter, used his low center of gravity to plow back defensive linemen. The quarterback, Luke Rasmussen, the grandson of the founder, was six feet, three inches. But perhaps most of all, Faith Baptist had speed.

A. C. Swadling, a wide receiver and defensive back, darted around the field so fast his teammates called him the Missile. Despite his slight frame—he was five feet, eleven inches and 150 pounds—he was a punishing tackler who could slam much larger players to the turf by throwing his body at them. A junior, he showed passion for the game, claiming to have woken up at 5:00 a.m. every day since he was a freshman, lifting weights and running routes in his quest for a championship ring.

Parker Mills, the son of a handyman, was the team's star running back. On weekends, Mills waited tables at a restaurant in Malibu frequented by Hollywood stars and their families. On the field he had good size and speed. At six feet, one inch and 185 pounds, Mills ran a 4.6 in the forty-yard dash, wheels that would help get him around the edges for big gains.

Unlike the Cubs, Faith Baptist met every day of Thanksgiving week, even sneaking in a practice on Thanksgiving morning. And just like the Avalon Lancers, the Faith Baptist Contenders had seen the media coverage of the Cubs. They were eager to flip the script on the media darlings of the moment.

18

Finishing with a Bang

Going into the championship game, the Cubs' hard-hitting running back, linebacker, and noseguard, Cody Metzner, had been skeptical of a big turnout two days after Thanksgiving. Many people were away. But on the evening of Saturday, November 27, 2021, as the Cubs entered the John W. North High School stadium, they looked up into the stands and saw a sea of red shirts. The school had sold 2,362 tickets before the game, and hundreds more spectators had bought tickets at the door. The line to enter the stadium went around the block. More than fifty reporters, television correspondents, camera operators, and photographers had shown up. The media list was an alphabet soup of the country's top networks: ABC, NBC, FOX, CNN, ESPN, all had reporters at the stadium. Two representatives from Tom Brady's production company were there. The greatest quarterback in the history of professional football was interested in making a movie about the team.

When Cody looked closely into the stands, he saw that many of the spectators were signing. "I knew the deaf community had come out for us," he said.

David Figueroa, a junior who played defensive end, found it

hard to keep his eyes on the field. "I couldn't stop looking at the crowd," he said. In the span of a few weeks the Cubs had gone from an obscure team playing on a torn-up field to a championship contender followed by television cameras and playing to a crowd of thousands. There were still seats left on the Faith Baptist side of the field, but they were filling up fast.

As spectators found their seats in the stands, a television reporter stood on the sidelines ready to interview Nancy Hlibok Amann, the superintendent of CSDR.

Hlibok Amann was royalty in the deaf community. Her parents had been featured in a slightly patronizing 1973 *New York Times* article that fawned over how two deaf parents, a civil engineer and a sociologist, could live a "full and active life." The couple's four children would do much more than that. Nancy's brother Gregory would spearhead the Deaf President Now movement at Gallaudet University, a protest that became a seminal moment in deaf history; students demanded that their administrators be deaf as well. Another brother, Bruce, would become the first deaf actor to play a main role in a Broadway production, *Runaways,* in 1978. Nancy's third brother, Steve, was hired as the first deaf stockbroker at Merrill Lynch and would rise to vice president at the financial firm.

In a bright red shirt adorned with the logo of a snarling bear cub, Nancy watched as the television reporter's questions were interpreted into ASL.

"What a special night for the Cubs football team, but also for this community," the reporter said. "What does it mean for this school district and this school?" He pointed his microphone in Nancy's direction for a response.

Nancy looked down at the microphone, smiled, and signed, "I don't think I need that. Feel free to keep that for yourself." It was an awkward moment, but one that underlined what a pioneering night it was: a deaf team was vying for a trophy that had always been won by hearing teams.

"We are going to finish this evening with a bang," she said. "I hope that this game sends a strong message worldwide."

The Cubs' four captains—Enos Zornoza, Trevin Adams, Christian Jimenez, and Jory Valencia—walked to midfield, their arms locked together, for the coin toss. CSDR won and chose to receive.

The Cubs' first possession of the game saw a series of aggressive throws by Trevin Adams, including a twenty-yard catch by Jory Valencia but a rare dropped pass by Felix Gonzales that would have put them on the doorstep of the end zone. On fourth down, an errant throw by Trevin halted the drive. Faith Baptist took over, and three plays later Luke Rasmussen, the Faith quarterback, heaved a long ball to a receiver in the end zone and connected. Faith Baptist had drawn first blood. With a successful two-point conversion to A. C. Swadling it was 8–0.

These first two drives set a pattern for the Cubs in the first quarter. They went nowhere on the next drive, and Faith, once they got the ball, scored again. Parker Mills, the Faith running back, ran around the edge, something he would do again and again, sprinting to the end zone.

By the end of the first quarter, the Cubs looked outmatched. Their possessions had been lamentable: a turnover on downs, two punts, and a fumble. Throughout the quarter, Trevin Adams had been under relentless pressure, his line failing to protect him for more than a couple of seconds each play. Faith Baptist, by contrast, had scored every time they had the ball. With the second quarter about to begin, it was Faith Baptist 28, Cubs 0.

Keith Adams huddled with his defeated-looking squad. He decided to go for a desperation play. It was fourth and ten deep in their own territory, and Adams told the team they were going for it. Felix lined up as running back, standing to the right of Trevin. Jory was wide right. The defense was playing Jory very soft; they knew that all they had to do was stop the Cubs before the first-down marker. At the snap, Jory took three long strides, making it look as if he were planning to run deep. But on the third step he pivoted to a stop so abruptly that his left foot sent up a spray of tiny rubber pellets from the artificial turf. He faced Trevin and was wide open but still five yards short of the first down. Trevin threw the ball high over the outstretched arms of the Faith Baptist linebacker, and Jory made a basketball move, leaping into the air, arms outstretched. With the defense already converging on Jory, it looked sure that Faith Baptist would make their fourth-down stop, extending the Cubs' misery. But as soon as Jory landed on the ground, he pitched the ball back to Felix, who was streaming out of the backfield. Felix grabbed the gently thrown toss with one hand—his left hand—and tucked it into his chest. Because he was a southpaw, the play was perfectly designed for him. He never slowed down. The play needed perfect rhythm, and the Cubs had it. Felix had no blockers in front of him, but he didn't need any. He went sixty yards for the touchdown, easily beating three of the Contenders' speediest players in a footrace.

The Cubs then kept up their momentum, stopping Faith Baptist on the next drive, forcing the Contenders' first punt. CSDR went fully airborne with Jory Valencia hauling in four straight passes. On the fourth completion, an eleven-yard gain, Jory was brought down by A. C. Swadling, who tried to punch the ball out of Jory's chest when he was already on the ground, drawing a fifteen-yard penalty for a personal foul. From the Cubs' side of the field, it looked like a back-alley slug to the gut. The crowd booed what they saw as poor sportsmanship.

Swadling was a tackling machine for Faith Baptist. His personal defensive philosophy turned on both the physical and the psychological. He would fly down the field, launch his body, and spear defenders' legs with his shoulders. He had learned that if you hit the inside of a runner's shins, you could sweep them away without them having any chance at a stiff-arm. He would psych himself up for every game by inventing ideas about his opponents. "Whoever I'm tackling, I put my problems onto them—'You are the reason my grandma is dead!'—something crazy in my head and I just attack them like a lion. 'You just stole my mom's money! I'm going to go get it for her.'" It was a somewhat unique way of operating, but it appeared to work. By the time the night was over, Swadling would tally eighteen tackles in the game. His philosophy seemed in sync with Faith Baptist's overall approach. "The more aggressive person wins," Swadling said.

But on this drive Swadling had been too aggressive. His penalty had put the Cubs on the ten-yard line. Adams rolled out right and connected with Jory Valencia—again—in the end zone. In a single drive, Jory had caught five passes.

There were roars and hollers from the CSDR fans in the bleachers as the crowd rose to their feet. It felt like the beginnings of a comeback. A pass caught by Felix Gonzales gave the Cubs two more points. The score was 28–16 with 8:45 left in the first half.

Kaveh Angoorani's defense needed a stop if the Cubs wanted to keep up their momentum. With Faith Baptist now on offense, Cubs fans stomped their feet on the bleachers so forcefully that a television reporter said it felt like a magnitude 5 earthquake.

From their own thirty-yard line, Faith Baptist tried a running play up the middle that got them five yards. But after the runner was down and the whistle blown, a Faith Baptist running back, D. J. McDaniel, shoved Trevin Adams so forcefully that he sent Trevin flying to the turf, his head whipping to the ground. McDaniel, clearly emotional, then began shoving his own players. A very physical game had turned bitter. McDaniel was called for unsportsmanlike conduct. Despite a subsequent long run down the sidelines by Parker Mills, the Cubs stopped Faith Baptist and got the ball back.

The Cubs started at their twenty-five-yard line. Once again, the Faith Baptist defense shot through the offensive line unimpeded. But this time it was intentional, a screen pass. Trevin lobbed the ball over the rushing defenders to the waiting hands of Jory Valencia, who fought for a forty-yard gain. After being tackled at the Faith Baptist ten-yard line, he limped off the field with a foot injury. Without Jory on the field, the Cubs pressed for the end zone. Scrambling to avoid the rush, Trevin launched a pass to Felix Gonzales, who was bracketed by two defenders. The throw landed exactly where it needed to. It was another Cubs touchdown. But it had come at a cost. Kaden Adams, who had been blocking for his brother in the pocket, went down, clutching his ankle. He would nurse it for a few minutes on the sidelines and reenter the game, playing for the duration. Stunningly, an X-ray would later reveal the ankle had been broken. He played through the pain.

With 5:39 left in the first half, the score was 28–22. The Cubs were battered, but trailing by only one touchdown.

19

"No Hope Left"

Give me the ball! Give me the ball!"
Parker Mills didn't understand why Faith Baptist had been trying long passes when their running game, especially to the outside, had been working so well. So now he implored his coaches on the sidelines, "Give me the ball!"

Mills got his wish. Running behind his 250-pound center, he curved around the perimeter to the left and sprinted around the edge. Tired Cubs defenders chased him down and then got up slowly from the turf. Faith Baptist was grinding down the Cubs' defense. With their energized running game, Faith answered the Cubs' scoring binge with a touchdown. And then on the next drive they intercepted a short pass intended for Felix Gonzales and scored again. After the play was over, Trevin and Felix argued over who was to blame, but it didn't matter. Within two minutes, Faith Baptist had scored twice.

On the Contenders' last drive before the half, Parker Mills ran the ball for ten yards and then for forty yards. With less than a minute remaining, Tracy Bryden, the six-foot, eight-inch tight end, caught a short pass and walked into the end zone. Parker Mills capped off the drive with a run up the middle for the two-point conversion. Faith Baptist finished the half leading 50–22.

The Cubs' locker room at halftime might as well have been a field hospital. Cody Metzner looked around and saw glassy-eyed players limping and tending to various parts of their aching bodies.

"I thought it was over in that moment," Cody said. "Everyone in the room had the same feeling, but no one said it. With all these injuries, there was just no way. I could see it in their faces; they had already given up. They had no hope left."

As an indicator of how the rest of the game went, nothing better symbolized the Cubs' struggles than the third play of the second half. Faith Baptist, which had received the third-quarter kickoff, had a stout offensive line, and Parker Mills had been running behind them on a number of plays. But on this play, he ran straight into the teeth of the Cubs' defense, barely assisted by any blocking. From the backfield he ran past David Figueroa, who seemed unable to pivot his body to attempt a tackle. Trevin, the team's best and hardest-hitting tackler, got only a single hand on the runner. Mills then shed a feeble attempt by Cody Metzner to grab him around the waist; he shook off Phillip Castaneda's arms around his ankles and burst away from Christian Jimenez. As he reached the goal line, he stiff-armed Felix Gonzales. It was a twenty-five-yard blast through a defense that had been one of the best in the league all season. Now the Cubs looked, as one of their coaches put it, as if they were walking in quicksand.

Christian Jimenez would later recall the feeling of mental and physical exhaustion at that point in the game. He and other players on the team had not recovered from the very physical game against Avalon a week earlier. "In the beginning we were fighting hard," he said of the championship. "But then I just gave up. I knew we weren't going to get the win."

David Figueroa looked back on Mills's twenty-five-yard touch-down run, and said it summed up the weakness of the whole season:

From those first days at practice in August, the team had shed some of their pandemic weight and sloth, but they had not spent enough time in the weight room. They were still not in good enough shape to play four quarters of a highly competitive game. "It was the first time going up against a team that had that much strength, agility, and speed," Figueroa said. "We were overconfident for sure."

The coup de grâce for the Cubs came on the next set of downs. From the shotgun, Trevin Adams called for the snap and then ran for three yards before he was met by two Faith defenders. Fighting for extra inches, Trevin hit the ground hard, his head and body bouncing off the turf. After being helped to his feet by his teammates, Trevin took a few steps and then knelt down. He was out for the rest of the game with a concussion, for the second time in all his years playing football.

Kaden Adams, his broken ankle heavily taped, took over for his brother. Jory Valencia was out of the game with an ankle injury, and his teammates were emotionally depleted. On the first play, Kaden threw a pass that went straight into the hands of—who else?—Parker Mills, who ran the ball back for a touchdown.

The Cubs did not score a single point in the third and fourth quarters. In an acknowledgment of how outmatched they were, Keith Adams asked the referees to run the clock—not stopping it at the end of each play. The final score, 74–22, was a humiliation in full view of what seemed like countless cameras and fans. Faith Baptist had done to the Cubs what the Cubs had been doing to their adversaries all season long. It was the Cubs' turn to feel the heartache of a blowout loss.

At the final whistle, the Cubs walked dejectedly to the sidelines. Felix Gonzales was inconsolable and could not be persuaded to huddle with the team. His teammates took a knee, tears streaking down their cheeks.

When a game is so lopsided through the second half, fans often trickle away into the night. But the grandstands had remained full.

At the end of the contest, the Cubs' supporters raised their hands above their heads and clapped.

"I'm so proud of my school," said Patricia Davis, the alumna who had enrolled at CSDR in its very first year. "Those boys," she said, "they worked so hard. I'm here to support them."

20

Unfinished Business

On February 13, 2022, at SoFi Stadium in Inglewood, California, seventy thousand fans roared before the coin toss of Super Bowl LVI between the Los Angeles Rams and the Cincinnati Bengals. Standing on the field before a television audience of millions, Trevin, Christian, Jory, and Enos represented their team, and deaf atheletes writ large. The cameras panned across their faces and announced their presence. It was a joyous milestone. The Super Bowl also featured deaf performers at halftime, part of what the NFL said was a focus on inclusion. A spokeswoman for the league said the Cubs and deaf performers had been invited because they were "defying stereotypes."

And yet the boys' quest still felt very much incomplete. The sting of defeat had carried over into the Christmas holidays, and then into the New Year. They had made it to a championship game, and that was a pioneering first. They had the plaque on the wall in the locker room to prove it. But what they wanted more than anything was not the silver medal.

Immediately after the game, Keith Adams had assembled his players. "I'm so proud of all of you guys," he told them. "With this we walk away with higher self-esteem. We had this one loss. But look at all the wins." He finished with a rallying cry for the next season. "This is unfinished business," he told them.

The team knew they would lose one of their stars, Enos, who was graduating. But Trevin, Felix, Jory, Cody, Christian, and David were all juniors and would be back, not to mention the younger players. Coach Adams managed to persuade Kaveh Angoorani to delay his retirement by six months, just enough time for another run at the championship.

From the start, their offseason looked different from the previous year's. The players met in the weight room through spring and summer, and Galvin Drake never failed to remind them that it was the lack of stamina and strength that had foiled their championship dreams. A year earlier, Galvin had to pester his players to work out. Now they came voluntarily—eagerly even. They were competing with one another as they lifted, driven by the sour memory of the Thanksgiving week loss. "The flashback of losing the championship was traumatizing," Galvin said.

.   .   .

During spring and summer vacations, players visited their extended families, who wanted to hear about their history-making season. Alfredo Baltazar, who would be a sophomore the next season, traveled to Mexico to the village of his parents and grandparents. He was the only deaf person in his family and communicated through basic gestures and using his phone, typing out messages and handing the device back and forth. For the members of his family who did not speak English, including his grandparents, who had a farm with goats, chickens, and horses, he would run the text through Google Translate and get phrases in Spanish. He showed them videos of news broadcasts and a translation of the *New York Times* article about how these underdogs had made it to the playoffs. Baltazar was the first person in his family to play football, a game growing in popularity in Mexico. He wanted to show his family how well he was doing—and that a deaf team could play and win big. "We are so proud of you," his grandmother told him.

Baltazar sported short hair and square-framed black glasses, the kind you might see in the store window of an optician with a somewhat fashionable clientele. He had a gentle demeanor that didn't jibe with the hand-to-hand combat he would wage in the trenches of the offensive line. The previous season he had been mostly second string, the coaches feeling he was not ready as a starter. In the November championship game, Baltazar had stood on the sidelines watching as the Cubs were routed, the offensive line offering little protection. It had left him with a helpless feeling. He wanted to be out there. "That's when I really decided I wanted to become dedicated," he said.

He took to the weight room at school and gradually increased his bench presses from 100 pounds to 170. He ran up Mount Rubidoux, a cactus-covered hill in downtown Riverside that had a network of paved walking trails that spiraled to the top. It was the Riverside equivalent of the steps at the Philadelphia Museum of Art, the ones made famous by Rocky Balboa.

Football had given Baltazar a sense of purpose and identity, especially inside his family. His mother had been impressed by his more muscular physique. "Wow, keep going!" she told him. The limited communication inside his family only made the bonds with his football teammates that much stronger. He reveled in the brotherhood of the team. He committed himself to becoming a better football player.

21

"Full Sprints!"

If deafness were a shape, it would be round. On August 4, 2022, the Cubs' coaching staff met in Keith Adams's office in the athletic facility at CSDR. They positioned their chairs in a semicircle, the perfect configuration for a deaf meeting where everyone needed to be able to see one another. As they gathered, multiple conversations took place across the room at once without anyone straining to understand.

There was Kaveh Angoorani, who had restarted the clock to his retirement; Ken Watson, the seventy-year-old CSDR alumnus who said he felt like a grandfather to the players; and Michael Mabashov, a lanky athlete who had nearly gone professional in golf and now gave lessons to a deaf clientele in Southern California. Farther along the curved seating arrangement sat Kevin Croasmun, a social studies teacher at the school who was also the wrestling coach; Davis Nguyen, who helped the team with their equipment and whose parents had arrived from Vietnam as refugees; and Galvin Drake, the enforcer, who was still driving around campus blasting electronic music at full volume. Ryan Zarembka, another assistant coach, came in slightly late, fresh off a flight from Texas, where he had visited his family.

The room smelled as if someone had purchased the entire aisle of antiperspirants and deodorants at CVS and taken the caps off all at once. The coaches wore the various polyester name brands of the modern American sports apparel industry, sneakers with short socks, loose athletic shorts, and T-shirts.

There has been a movement over the past two decades to design facilities used by deaf people in architecturally appropriate ways. This might include spaces that could easily accommodate "conversation circles." Hallways would be wide enough so that groups of people could sign to one another as they walked; single file does not allow for ASL conversation. The corridors might be rounded so that people did not startle each other around sharp corners. The color schemes and lighting would be "visually quiet," allowing for signers to talk with each other and not strain their eyes.

Keith Adams's office, and the athletic facility in which it was located, had none of this. It was a standard-issue government building. He worked in a windowless cinder-block classroom, a very institutional setting with four banks of neon lights and white acoustic ceiling tiles. A dolly in the middle of the room carried foldable chairs, the kind you might see rolling past during coffee hour in the basement of a Methodist church. E-X-I-T glared in red letters from atop the doors. Inches from his desk, Coach Adams kept a hotel-room-sized refrigerator and a microwave oven, ensuring that he would never need to travel far for a snack. A buzzer sounded between periods, a noise that no one could hear. There were also speakers in the hallways that broadcast emergency messages. No one could hear those either. The staff in the athletic facility had rolled their eyes when the California agency that designed the building installed the speakers.

There *were* two concessions to deafness: a small screen in each classroom flashed "Class Ending," and the fire alarms came with flashing lights.

The coaches talked to one another about their summer vacations, how producers from Disney had reached out to interview them for the television series that the network planned to do on the team, how hot it was outside. Most important, they thought about where they were a year ago—herding a group of boys who were woefully out of shape—and wondered whether the players would be better prepared this year. They faced an added challenge this season: The Southern Section of the California Interscholastic Federation had changed the format for the playoffs, doing away with the two-tiered system for eight-man football. There was now only one championship game, no matter how big or small the school was.

Halfway through the meeting, the older coach, Ken Watson, piped in with a suggestion that they weigh the players before preseason training. Watson, who had spent his career working at the post office, was beloved on the team for one of his jokes. At the end of practices and after games he would ask the players to cheer loudly and then cup his hand to his ear. "I can't hear you!" he would say. The players would then scream at the top of their lungs. "I still can't hear you!" he would say.

At the meeting Watson also suggested they weigh the players after the preseason, to see if they had lost weight during the workouts. Everyone remembered how overweight some of the players had been the year before.

Keith shrugged off the idea. "Strength and speed, that's all that matters to me," he said.

After laying out the preseason schedule, the coaches adjourned for a late lunch at their favorite pizzeria. There they proceeded to take bets on how many players would vomit at the first conditioning practice later that evening.

·   ·   ·

"Full sprints! Full sprints!" signed Galvin Drake.

It was 7:00 p.m. and eighty-eight degrees but rapidly cooling down with a nice breeze. The Cubs were on the field in white shirts and black shorts. They could have been mistaken for cadets during basic training. In one corner, Kaveh Angoorani showed a crop of new defensive linemen how to swing their arms like windmills so they could get past their opponents on the line.

Coach Adams gathered another group of boys along the sidelines. "We are champions, right?" he asked them.

Adams walked around the field and tried starting the diesel generators that power the highway lights used to illuminate the field. A few of them couldn't be coaxed into firing up. Davis Nguyen, the equipment guru, prodded the engines and turned a crank that seemed to make the lights brighter. It was a new season, with the same old equipment. A sticker on the machines had the name WhisperWatt, but it seemed a misnomer. They were as loud as they were polluting, spewing fumes across the field. The new stadium that the governor had promised wouldn't be built for several years.

Just before 8:00 p.m., the players were running a drill when Cody Metzner flung off his helmet, walked gingerly beyond the sidelines, planted his left knee in the grass, and threw up.

"Take it easy," Kaveh Angoorani signed to him. The coaches would later disagree on how many players threw up that day. Kaveh had counted four and Coach Adams three. But the number, everyone agreed, revealed something important. Three or four: it was far fewer than the ten who had retched the year before.

.   .   .

The Cubs were one player short. Phillip Castaneda, their fierce running back and safety who had started out sleeping in his car in the Target parking lot, was on the sidelines at practice but not participating. In the late spring, the California Interscholastic Federation notified the team in an unexpected ruling that Phillip was ineligible to play. He had dropped out of school so many times that this would technically be his fifth year of high school. Academically, he was still taking courses normally reserved for freshmen or sophomores. He hadn't played football his freshman, sophomore, or junior year. But he was eighteen years old, and by his age and the number of years that he had been enrolled, he was now beyond eligibility. Keith Adams had gone to the federation offices to argue that he should be able to play because of his difficult family circumstances, but the officials didn't budge.

In the late spring, when Keith learned of the federation's decision, Phillip was hard to contact. He was once again absent from school for weeks at a time. And he wasn't answering his phone or his email. Keith went to the house near campus where Phillip had found a room and pounded on the door. When Phillip finally appeared, Keith conveyed the news to him and tried to persuade him to return to school. What's the point of coming back to school if I can't play football? Phillip replied.

Keith told him that his education was important and that he could serve as the team's manager. That arrangement worked out for a few weeks. Phillip would carry the water bottles and watch wistfully from the sidelines. But he was kicked off the team after he was caught going to the cannabis shop in the Target parking lot with four other players on the team. Although the legal minimum was twenty-one years old for recreational marijuana in California, Phillip had a doctor's note that allowed him to buy cannabis to treat anxiety. All along, Keith had been concerned that the dysfunction of Phillip's family, his father's drug use, and Phillip's spotty attendance in classes would rub off on other players. His fears had been realized with the trip to the pot shop. The four other players, mostly freshmen and sophomores, would be suspended for several weeks.

Until the very last game of the 2022 season, Phillip stuck with the team—but as a spectator. He watched from the bleachers as his former teammates pursued their quest for the championship.

22

"Be Hungry for It! Be Angry!"

As the preseason gathered steam, it was clear that this was a different team. The flab that had jiggled and protruded from underneath uniforms the previous year was trimmed. Galvin Drake, the master of the weight room and the bench press, put a number to the team's preparedness. The players had added forty pounds of strength, he calculated. Other coaches agreed. They were still teenagers, but losing the championship had brought wisdom. The players seemed more serious and mature.

Their preseason routines were governed on the field by the strict football regulations of California law. When concussions had become a major concern a decade earlier, the California legislature had passed a law that limited full-contact practices to twice a week. There were also more specific rules on what days in August practice could start and how much conditioning was required before the full contact could commence. The rules said explicitly that football cleats, helmets, and footballs were the only equipment allowed during the conditioning period. And the law defined full-contact practice as one that "involves collisions at game speed where players execute tackles and other activity that is typical of an actual tackle football game." You almost had to be an attorney to understand all the rules. But it was all in the interest of making the sport safer.

Before their first practice playing with full pads, the players voted for their team captains, selecting Trevin, Jory, Felix, and Kaden. Then, at 6:30 p.m., they gathered on the field under a beautiful orange sunset. Michael Mabashov led the players in a fumble drill and told them to "eat some grass" as they scrambled for the ball. "Be hungry for it! Be angry! Show effort!" he signed.

They lined up for a two-on-two drill, a ballcarrier and blocker facing two tacklers. At the coaches' signal the play would start. When it was Felix Gonzales's turn, he lined up as the ballcarrier, darted past the first defender, and then leaped into the air, hurdling the second would-be tackler. The whole team jumped toward the sky, arms raised, as if he had caught the winning touchdown in the Super Bowl. They howled in admiration of his acrobatic, tackle-evading leap.

·   ·   ·

During breaks at practice, Andrei Voinea, a senior who had sprouted in the offseason and was now, at six feet, four inches, the tallest player on the team, tried to coax younger players to help him practice his snap. Voinea was the team's backup center, and he felt as if he had a lot of catching up to do. A few years earlier he had transferred from a hearing school that had no sports teams. With the Cubs, a team that began most of their plays from the shotgun, perfecting the snap was especially important.

On and off the field, Voinea was an unboastful young man who had a lot to boast about. Although he was not a starter, with his size and heft—he weighed around 240 pounds—the coaches wished nothing more than for him to become a first-string lineman. But on the cusp of turning seventeen, he was also a formidable video game programmer in his spare time. He had helped design the animations for games on the Roblox platform popular with preteens. When pressed, he would mention some of his creations. He had done the animations for parts of the game *ESCAPE Miss Marie's Library*, a game that had been played millions of times and was one of the most popular on the platform. But he kept his accomplishments mostly to himself, and few of his teammates were aware of his programming skills.

At times he saw real life through the lens of his video game programming, he said. In football, it helped him conceptualize plays. "I feel like I am looking at the field from above, and I can move the pieces around," he said. When he collaborated with other programmers online, they would ask to video chat to discuss certain projects. He would explain to them that he was deaf. Without fail, his online colleagues would be very surprised. "No, you're making that up. Are you serious?" they would say. And then they got over it. Voinea's professional goal was to become an animator for Disney.

His parents lived in Burbank but were from Romania originally, and his household was bilingual. He communicated with American Sign Language, and his parents, both deaf, spoke to each other in Romanian sign language. The two were not mutually comprehensible. Throughout his childhood, his family traveled back to his grandparents' farm in Romania for long vacations among the apple orchards. He watched his grandparents slaughter chickens and helped tend to the other animals.

He lived this split-screen life, between the freeways, the smog, and the conveniences of Los Angeles and the poor and rugged countryside of his grandparents' subsistence farming in eastern Europe. During his earliest visits to the farm in Romania, his grandparents did not have piped water in the house, and he had to walk half a mile to fill pails from the river. The family had a battered car, but they used it sparingly, preferring instead to deploy their horse-drawn cart around the property. "It was such a different experience," Andrei says matter-of-factly. "There was dirt and mud everywhere."

When he returned to Los Angeles for school, he found himself perpetually frustrated. At home, communication was easy. But if he didn't understand something in class, he couldn't just ask the teacher. Everything had to go through his sign-language interpreter. And if the interpreter was late or absent, as sometimes happened, Andrei was on his own.

Some of his hearing classmates would try to sign or gesture, and he appreciated that. But he found the interactions very limiting. "We could only talk about very, very basic things," he said. "I wasn't able to joke and laugh with them. I felt very isolated."

He transferred to CSDR in the eighth grade, and initially he was startled at the speed of signed conversations. He could talk about anything with anyone. He forged deeper friendships with his new deaf friends and joined the football team.

Now, in his senior year, the accomplished computer programmer found himself perfecting the art of launching a ball between his legs. Michael Mabashov was hopeful for Voinea's prospects and was encouraged to see him constantly practicing snaps. But he wanted to fix one more thing about Voinea. He was too nice. "You have to find that aggression," Mabashov told him.

.　　　.　　　.

At the end of practice, Keith Adams gathered his players to offer an assessment. In less than three weeks they would play their season opener against Chadwick School, a tough competitor from a wealthy coastal area of Los Angeles County. Chadwick would be a difficult game, maybe the hardest of the regular season. The two teams had never played each other, but Keith urged his players to study game film from the previous season. He also told them he had been happy with what he saw on the field that day. "I liked the physical aggression," he said.

Galvin Drake admonished the players to improve their diets. "How long is football season? Four months. That's it. I challenge all of you to give up soda for four months. It's really bad for you, and it makes you cramp up."

And Michael Mabashov told the players he appreciated that they went all out in their sprints and drills despite the heat. He thanked them for their enthusiasm going to the turf in the fumble-recovery drills. "You finally ate some grass," he said. "It put a smile on my face."

Preseason had come to a close. The new season—and a chance to play again for a championship—beckoned.

23

"They Think We Are Nothing"

J osh Goodman couldn't sit still. The opening game—the big game—was a week away, and his mind was churning with scenarios. A star running back, receiver, and kicker for the Chadwick School, he would be playing the California School for the Deaf, Riverside. It would be the first time that he and any of his teammates played a deaf school. The game had preoccupied Goodman all summer long. He was jumpy even when sitting in his car thinking about it. In past seasons he would get so nervous before taking the field that he would vomit, sometimes repeatedly. He would do the same before this game.

The first game of any season often fills players and coaches with apprehension. But this contest, Chadwick School versus CSDR, loomed even larger. Both sides badly wanted to chart a path to the championship and felt the pressure to win. Both head coaches considered it one of the hardest games on their schedules, even though the school year was barely under way. For either team, there would be no middling opponent to test out new plays, no way of assessing how rookie players would really fare in their new positions, and no season momentum to prepare and lift them up for the big test. They would not really know the strength of their rosters, not know how well their boys had memorized the playbook, until the game clock started just before sunset on a bumpy field in Riverside, California. To paraphrase Mike Tyson: In football, as in life, everything is just theory and conjecture until you get punched in the mouth.

The game was all the more anticipated when the Chadwick players learned that it would be captured by a professional NFL film crew. The cameramen would be there to gather footage for a show about the Cubs, and Coach Adams in particular. Chadwick wanted nothing more than to dominate their opponents' highlight reel. The Chadwick players did not know—and many would not even know until after the game was over—that Kurt Warner, the Hall of Fame quarterback who had led the St. Louis Rams to their first-ever Super Bowl win two decades earlier, would be standing on the sidelines studiously watching each play, gray-haired but still showing the athletic bearing and posture of an NFL quarterback.

The Chadwick School is located on the affluent Palos Verdes peninsula that protrudes into the Pacific Ocean just south of Manhattan and Redondo Beaches. It's an area that epitomizes coastal California, with horse clubs and surfers and bluffs that give way to the ocular infinity of the Pacific Ocean. Squint past the blue-green swells and through the haze that hovers over the ocean and you might imagine Japan, five thousand miles away. Along the coast are mansions and mature trees with elegant canopies that seem big enough to offer shade to a full symphonic orchestra. Nearby there's a Trump golf course and hiking trails that snake along the ocean.

The game in Riverside would bring together two very different schools. Chadwick was an elite private school with a forty-five-acre hilltop campus framed by bright red bougainvillea bushes and homes that, on average, go for well above $2 million. The school cannot host night games because neighbors opposed installing lights around the playing fields, lest they pollute the sweeping views of Greater Los Angeles. Chadwick's annual tuition is $44,000, not including textbooks and the $1,500 matriculation fee for new students. The school was founded in 1935, and the ranks of alumni range from the actress Liza Minnelli to the former No. 1–ranked tennis star Lindsay Davenport. It was a place that over the years had hosted the children of the Hollywood glitterati. The school played a cameo part in the movie *Mommie Dearest,* the embittered tale of Christina Crawford's childhood as the daughter of the Hollywood star Joan Crawford.

As for football, Chadwick was known for being disciplined and successful. The previous year they had won eight of their ten games, and the two games they lost had been close. Chadwick had not had a losing record in nearly two decades, before any of the current players were born. They were not known for being physically imposing; at the start of the 2022 season, the team had no player heavier than 190 pounds. They were long and lanky and a little light in the hips, as their coach noted. But what they lacked in size, they made up for in a regimented execution of their playbook. The coaching staff in recent years had been drawn in large part from officers who had attended the U.S. Air Force Academy. The coaches taught the Chadwick players to stand up straight, "yes, sir," "no, sir," toes on the line. "We want our toes right on the line, not over the line, not behind the line," Coach Jordan Ollis would bark. Ollis had spent a year at the Air Force Academy before transferring to Brevard, a small private college in the lush mountains of North Carolina where they filmed *The Hunger Games.* He had kept his southern accent and sprinkled his speech with "y'alls."

In the weeks before the game, he and his players discussed deafness and how it might affect the game. They were intrigued at how the Cubs' communication system worked. "Orally communicating is such an important part of our game," Ollis said. "It is interesting to see how effective they can be without saying one word."

Playing a deaf team would strip Chadwick of one of their specialties, getting other teams penalized by jumping offside. Chadwick had succeeded in past seasons in confounding opponents by mixing up their snap count of "Blue! Down! Set! Hike!" They could start the play on just "Blue!" or "Set!" Or they would use a silent count, positioning themselves on the line and starting the play wordlessly. But when they looked at film of the Cubs, they saw that none of this would work: The Cubs almost never jumped offside. The deaf players were focused exclusively on the movement of the ball.

Ollis told his players that they should know that their deaf opponents might continue playing after the whistle was blown. He urged them to be understanding.

"There might be a situation where someone on their team is blocking you or going hard and you hear the whistle and they keep blocking," the coach said. "We are going to be compassionate when that happens. We're going to understand that they didn't hear it." It was genteel advice that would evaporate once the players hit the field and the violence of the game carried its inevitable sting.

But Ollis, his players, and anyone else involved with the team seemed clear-eyed about what they were up against: a team very hungry for a win, a team that had gone to the championship game nine months earlier, and a team that looked bigger and stronger than last year. This was football.

Jeff Mercer, the director of the middle school at Chadwick whose twin boys, Josh and Dylan, were linebackers on the team, put it this way before the game: "This idea that there is this auditory impairment, that somehow this is going to limit them—that's crazy. We are going to go down there, and they are going to be ready to smash us in the mouth." His words would prove prescient for what turned out to be a very physical game.

On the afternoon of Friday, August 26, the Chadwick players and coaches boarded a tall black luxury coach with CORPORATE COACH CHARTER written in bright red. And if the vehicle itself did not make it clear, there was further explicit description: "Transportation with Elegance."

The boys wore dress shirts, ties, and slacks. Some had sport coats, as if it were Eton or Harrow they were traveling to, not Riverside. Their journey, around seventy miles, would take them down a series of jumbo-sized freeways, going ever farther inland. A trip that would take an hour and fifteen minutes in the dead of night, when a motorist could glide down the ribbons of pavement like a Boeing zipping to takeoff, dragged on for nearly three hours in the clogged Friday afternoon traffic.

They were heading into the Inland Empire, past warehouses and strip malls and into the heat. The Pacific coast and the inland areas of California operate with such extreme meteorological remoteness from each other that you might have to drive thousands of miles in other parts of the country in order to get the same differences in temperature. But a jaunt across California's microclimates can easily swing the temperature by thirty degrees. When they boarded the bus at Chadwick, it was in the mid-eighties. When they stepped off the bus late that afternoon in Riverside, it was a stifling hundred degrees.

The Cubs, for their part, had spent the afternoon relaxing. Dismissal from class was early on Fridays to allow time for boarding students at the school to return home for the weekend.

As was their ritual, the boys gathered in one of the dormitories and played foosball, watched television, lounged on couches, scanned their phones.

Two players, both offensive linemen, seemed especially pensive. Ricardo Terrazas and Alfredo Baltazar would both be starters, Baltazar for the first time. Both had impressed coaches in the preseason with their dedication to becoming better football players and had won the starting jobs on the offensive line after showing grit during the season's first scrimmages.

Baltazar, the player who had visited his grandparents in Mexico in the offseason, played the crucial position of left tackle, where he defended the quarterback's so-called blind side. When the quarterback dropped back and faced the right-hand sideline to pass (all three of the team's quarterbacks were right-handed), Baltazar would have to be there to protect him. Terrazas played center, charged with the team's unique, silent snap of the ball. The coaches hoped that the two boys would address one of the most glaring deficiencies of the previous season: the woeful lack of blocking by the offensive line.

Baltazar and Terrazas had a lot in common. They were both the only deaf people in their families and had limited communication with their parents and siblings growing up. They both came from Mexican backgrounds, where soccer, not football, was the favorite sport to watch and play.

But CSDR did not have a varsity soccer team, and eventually, after many years attending the Riverside campus (Terrazas had been at the school since he was one year old), they had turned to football.

Terrazas felt a sense of urgency as the season began. It was his senior year. He had to commit to football, he said. He had to play hard. "Basically invest everything that I've got," he said as his teammates played foosball in the dormitory. "Basically beat my body up until my season is over. That's all I'm thinking about."

Terrazas has a way of smiling boyishly as his hands furiously produce biting words that seem counter to his happy facial expressions. In the hours before the game, he described being moved by the powerful combination of feeling underestimated and looked down on.

He had researched the Chadwick School on the internet and seen slickly produced videos of a perfectly manicured campus, of smiling students in theatrical productions and on playing fields, making pottery and playing in an orchestra.

"Some rich-kid private school," he concluded. The contrast

between the Chadwick campus life he had seen online—the glossy catalog photos that private schools used to entice parents—and his own life verged on caricature. His father was a housepainter, and his mother worked in a warehouse. His brother had taken up boxing as a way to ward off bullying.

And even though Terrazas had never been to the Chadwick campus, nor had he ever met one of their students, the game stirred a sense of aggrievement inside him, not just about differences in wealth, but about his deafness and the way that he thought the world saw him.

"They think we are nothing; they think we are not a threat," he said. The opposite was true, in fact, as illustrated by the nervousness of Josh Goodman and his coach. But this was Terrazas's imagined adversary, and if it helped rile him up for the game, so be it.

"They always think we are not capable because we are deaf," Terrazas said more generally. "And I'm going to show them that it's not true. I'm going to show them that I can hit you just as hard as you can hit us. I'll prove you wrong."

Almost as soon as he had finished his thoughts, word spread that it was lunchtime, a trip to Riverside Plaza, the local strip mall, for sustenance. The boys abandoned their foosball games, jumped off the couches, and piled into white vans outside, ready to take them to the pizzerias, delis, and fast-food joints that would deliver them the calories that their bodies could never get enough of.

They took over half of the tables at the Blaze pizzeria and chewed their way through their pregame pies, lighting up the room with their bright scarlet jerseys. They were regulars at Blaze, and the staff and clientele showed no surprise that a group of deaf athletes had taken over an entire swath of the restaurant and were signing to one another enthusiastically. CSDR had been in Riverside longer than most businesses in the city, and store clerks were often unfazed when deaf customers approached them, quick to produce their mobile phones and type out questions—for here or to go? In some cases, the clerks knew some basic ASL.

At the middle tables were many of the team's stars: Jory, Trevin, Cody, Christian Jimenez. And when everyone was nearly done eating, Felix Gonzales, always the nonconformist, came strolling into the place wearing a white singlet and slides, the only player not in uniform.

The stars discussed their research and their hunches: Chadwick in previous years had fielded some big dudes, but this year they had lost all their players of size. In a moment of cocky confidence, Jory pointed to his quarterback and running back and signed Felix's name. "Look at the talent we have," Valencia said. "We can beat them."

Their coach was not so sure. Coach Adams saw in his players what he thought was a touch of hubris after the last season.

"You know, they think, 'I'm such a great player, blah, blah, blah,'" the coach said in his office before the Chadwick game. "You can't just half-ass it; that's what we're really trying to emphasize. For us to get to the championships, every single player needs to be good."

The coach went down the list of his concerns. Chadwick was very well coached, they had worked out almost all summer, they had a very good quarterback and talented wide receivers. Yes, some of Chadwick's biggest players had graduated and were no longer with the team, but it was the first game of the season, so Adams had no film to evaluate what their new line might look like. The coach did not share his star players' confidence, or at least he would not admit to it. He guessed that the game would be won in the trenches, "our linemen against their linemen." As he would before each game, he had made pancakes in his office for the linemen the evening before the game. Carbs and corn syrup might help give them a little more energy.

There would be another concern for the coaches before the

game: the distractions of having three NFL cameramen roaming the locker room, tracking them as they discussed strategy and had their ankles taped. The cameramen wanted to choreograph some of the pregame shots.

The pregame speeches were to be captured on film, and Trent Cooper, the director of the *NFL 360* episode that they were filming, sketched out the positioning of the protagonists. This is where the players would sit, where Coach Adams would stand in the narrow locker room. He laid out the scene on paper the way a coach might draw up a play.

It was agreed that Kurt Warner would talk to the team before the game, but the director made clear that he was counting on Adams to produce some pregame poetry.

"I want him, not Kurt, giving the best speech of his life," Cooper told the Cubs' interpreter, Mark Bayarsky.

The players stared at the cameramen and laughed at the Steadicam worn by one of them, a kind of exoskeleton that had levers and pulleys and looked as if it might be designed for the Mars rover. Hollywood had come to Riverside, and their locker room was the movie set.

The NFL team had wired Trevin Adams, the Cubs' quarterback, with a microphone and would do the same with the Chadwick QB. The purpose of Trevin's microphone was to pick up the ambient noises of the game—the crunching of shoulder pads, the crashing of helmets, and the oomph of hitting the turf. Kaveh Angoorani, the Cubs' defensive coordinator, enjoyed slapping Trevin Adams in the chest and watching the bars on the screen of the soundman's equipment flare.

Twenty minutes before the game was to start, the players sat on their benches in the locker room, and the cameramen took their places just as the director had planned. Kurt Warner strode in from the still-bright sunshine and flicked off his mirrored sunglasses, a floppy sun hat tucked into the back of his slacks. The previous summer, *American Underdog*, a film about Kurt Warner, had been released, showcasing the unlikely journey of a boy from Burlington, Iowa, from undrafted college quarterback, to penniless grocery store clerk, to third-string NFL quarterback, and ultimately to the leader of a long-struggling St. Louis Rams team that put on what became known as the Greatest Show on Turf. Warner had helmed a dazzling offense that led the Rams to victory at the Super Bowl. Kurt Warner knew something about being an underdog.

The starstruck Cubs players gazed up from their benches at this NFL Hall of Fame star. "How's everybody doing?" Warner said as the players' eyes shifted to Bayarsky, the team's interpreter. "Who's ready for some football?"

To the cheers of the players, Warner continued.

"I love this night. I love when the football season starts. And I wish that I had one more opportunity to put the pads on and play."

Warner offered the players three pieces of advice: "First, never take this for granted. Appreciate the fact that you get to play this game, that you get to go out there and compete against that other team. Second thing, never forget why you do what you do, why you play this game, why you love this game. Put a smile on your face. Enjoy the process. There's going to be ups and downs, but never forget why you play the game. And third thing: The greatest thing about football is that it's a team sport. We get to do this together. Right? All of us. There's going to be highs and lows. There's going to be times we have to pick our teammates up. There's going to be times we have to encourage our teammates. There are going to be times when we celebrate!"

At this point Trevin Adams stood up and ran up and down the benches, riling up the players. When he sat back down, Warner concluded: "That's what this game is all about. I'm excited to watch you guys play tonight. Go out and put on a show. Have a blast. Good luck to you guys."

Next up was Coach Adams. This, the NFL film crew had instructed, was supposed to be the speech of his life. But an NFL Hall of Famer was a hard act to follow, and with the awkwardness of having Adams's words simultaneously interpreted into English by Bayarsky (for the benefit of Warner and the NFL film crew), the speech was flat.

"All right," Bayarsky said, interpreting the end of Adams's speech while raising his voice to muster the same enthusiasm that had greeted Warner's words. "They want to beat us. Come on now. Don't let that happen. All right, play hard, all four quarters. It's not over till it's over. No mental mistakes, blocking has got to be good."

The team gathered at the entrance to the locker room and pounded on the walls as they did before every game, a thunderous thudding that seemed to shake the foundation of the locker room. Then they jogged into the evening sunshine.

.   .   .

On the field, Chadwick had been doing pregame warm-ups that looked straight out of the Air Force Academy. They clapped and stretched in perfect unison.

Right leg! Ready, stretch!

Left leg! Ready, stretch!

Helmets on! Yes, sir!

Back on their campus, Chadwick's home field was perfectly flat, manicured, and a deep chlorophyll green, with the sweeping view of Greater Los Angeles. It had terraced seating that had the feel of a Greek amphitheater. The white grid on the field was painted with precision. The red track that surrounded the field was smooth.

In Riverside, they had arrived at a thirsty field that had the feel of a vacant lot. At certain spots in the field, clouds of dust would rise with each passing player, the lines on the field were pale, and the largest divots had been filled in with dirt. The gridiron was surrounded by a neglected track and the bleachers that looked as if they had been sold on eBay after an old stadium was demolished. The school had looked into renting bleachers for the big game, but the cost, $50,000, was judged prohibitive.

As game time approached, the scene was disorienting for the Chadwick players for another reason: the national anthem was not part of the proceedings, and there was no announcer, nothing auditory except for the constant whoosh of cars passing on the nearby freeway, the squealing wheels of the mile-long freight trains that frequently passed on the tracks next to the school, and the diesel generators for the lights.

"Usually when you walk onto the field, there's music playing, you hear coaches screaming at the players," said Thomas Rosso, the Chadwick quarterback. "When we came out, everything was quiet. It was like us going out to a practice field. We had to bring our own energy."

Chadwick won the coin toss and elected to receive the ball.

Felix Gonzales, the Cubs' wide receiver who did double duty as kicker, teed up the ball on a patch of dirt. He raised his right arm, ran up to the ball, and then tapped it with his left foot, sending it just twelve yards down the field. The Cubs had started the season with an onside kick.

The kick sent Will Padian, the Chadwick safety, and Kory Jackson, a wide receiver, converging toward the ball. They collided and the ball slipped from Jackson's hands, rolling away from his grasp. For a fraction of a second the ball rolled away, waiting to be claimed. A stampede of red shirts dived for the ball. Ricardo Terrazas slid onto the turf, missing the ball by inches. Jory Valencia, the Cubs' wide receiver, dropped his lanky six-foot, three-inch frame directly onto the ball. The Cubs' sidelines erupted with hoots and hollers. The season was under way, and it had begun auspiciously for the Cubs.

What came next would be even more instructive on how the game would be played.

From their own thirty-six-yard line the Cubs lined up for their first offensive play. At the snap of the ball, a running play up the middle, Alfredo Baltazar, the newly muscled sophomore who had run up Mount Rubidoux all summer, charged into the Chadwick player across from him and never let up. By the end of the play, he had blocked him out of the picture. The casual fan watching the game and tracking the progress of the ball would have been unlikely to have even noticed. The eye was drawn to the quarterback plowing up the field behind his beefy running back. Yet for the Cubs' coaches, Baltazar's blocking would prove to be a sign of how the team had evolved. Baltazar had taken the Chadwick lineman out. It was exactly what the team had lacked the prior season.

On the third play of the Cubs' opening drive, Trevin Adams scored on a run capped by a dive into the end zone. That would be followed by a failed drive by Chadwick, giving the ball back to the Cubs and leading to another score. A second Chadwick drive ended in a blocked punt, with the Cubs recovering the ball on Chadwick's twenty-yard line. The Cubs would score a third time. By the end of the first quarter the home team was ahead 24–0.

The game was never close. It seemed that every time there was a hole, a possible opening, for Chadwick to gain a couple yards, the Cubs would come charging through, violently stopping their progress. On Chadwick's first offensive play, Baltazar and Metzner burst through the line. They tackled the senior Max Radmilovich before he could even look upfield, for a loss of seven yards. The play was emblematic of the whole game.

The Cubs would win the game, 54–16. Trevin Adams alone would have two hundred yards rushing, nearly as much as Chadwick's entire team would have rushing and passing.

It was a rout.

Josh Goodman ended the game with just nineteen yards in the

air and minus eight yards on the ground. He had carried the ball twice, both times for a loss. He was despondent and angry. Discussing the game the next day, he said he had been knocked around so much that the game was a blur. "This loss stinks," he said. "This was a wake-up call for our team. There's going to be a hunger that is three times what you saw last night."

During the game, the compassion that Coach Ollis had promised had evaporated. The Chadwick coaching staff and players harangued the referees for not picking up on what they said were obvious penalties. Coach Ollis had raged against the referees when plays extended beyond the whistle.

But just before boarding their executive coach back to the coast, Ollis walked to the office of Coach Adams to shake hands one more time.

"You were the better team tonight," Ollis said. "By far, no doubt."

24

Deaf Versus Deaf

Running more than a thousand miles up and down the West Coast, Interstate 5 winds across mountains and forges rivers from Tijuana to British Columbia. But the portion that crosses through California's Central Valley is one of the straightest pieces of pavement in America, passing so monotonously among almond orchards, industrial-sized cattle yards, and vast stretches of desert that steering wheels seem pointless. In the lingering summer heat of early September, a convoy of white vans sped down the interstate filled with student athletes whose excitement belied the tedium of the turnless stretch of freeway. The Cubs were headed north to the campus of their archrivals, the California School for the Deaf in Fremont. The Fremont school, across the bay from San Francisco, enrolls students from the northern half of California. Riverside takes the students from the Southlands, the dividing line being at San Luis Obispo. North versus South, an inevitable rivalry.

For the Cubs, the journey to Fremont would set in motion the first of three consecutive games against deaf schools, a rare trifecta of deaf versus deaf. The Cubs would play their two other deaf opponents, the Indiana School for the Deaf and the Florida School for the Deaf and the Blind, on their home field. These games against out-of-state teams were inserted into the Cubs' normal schedule of opponents from their Southern California league. Over the years, deaf schools had traveled across the country to play one another, giving a chance for the Riverside players to meet and mingle with fellow deaf athletes. The three games carried with them the potential for more than just casual bragging rights in the tight-knit deaf community: at the end of the season, a national deaf sports council would decide which deaf high school football team was the national champion based on performances across the country. The Cubs had been given that honor for the 2021 season and had the T-shirts to prove it. They had no intention of relinquishing their status as national deaf champions.

Playing deaf teams was an exhilarating switch for the Cubs. The vast majority of their opponents over the years had been hearing teams, which meant plenty of wordless glances through face masks and some attempts to communicate with very basic gesturing. But against Fremont and the other deaf teams the language barrier would evaporate. The last time the Cubs had played a deaf team had been three years earlier; so for many players, these would be their first deaf opponents. Coaches had organized social events with the opposing deaf teams on the evenings before the games. And during the games—theoretically—players could tell their opponents how much they admired a tackle or a leaping catch.

Kind words were not what Trevin Adams and his teammates had in mind as they readied themselves for the game against Fremont.

"Finally," he said, "we can trash-talk."

Insults flew in the game, and the best part, of course, was that the hearing referees were largely oblivious to the various and creative ways the players explored to tease and rag on one another.

Playing Fremont brought the potential for some conflicted emotions. Alexandero Morales, the Riverside alumnus who helped compile game statistics for the Cubs, remembered battling his own twin brother in the Fremont–Riverside game nearly a decade earlier, in 2013. The brothers had grown up in a foster home, and ultimately Alexandero was enrolled in Riverside while his brother Johnny went to Fremont. Fremont won the 2013 game, but Alexandero, nine years later, was still savoring the moment when, after his brother had caught a pass, he bore down on him. Alexandero had grabbed his twin, spun him to the ground, and yelled in celebration as he lay on top of him. "I'm watching you," Alexandero remembers signing to his twin. "You can't run away from me."

Fremont versus Riverside was that kind of rivalry, registering somewhere between fraternal camaraderie and fratricide. For the Adams boys, too, the game was very much a complicated family affair. Keith and Carol Adams had met at Fremont, and Carol's side of the family could count eight graduates from Fremont.

Yet despite these Adams family ties, it was clear where loyalties lay for father, mother, and sons. A few days earlier, Coach Adams had taped small squares of paper on his players' lockers in Riverside, each with the same set of dispiriting scores, the recent blowout losses that the Cubs had suffered at the hands of Fremont in past seasons. It was an embarrassing spreadsheet of crushing defeats:

60–0
42–0
62–0
65–0
65–0
59–0

Coach Adams had been wrong about one score. In the most recent game, the Cubs had actually managed to score eight points. But 59–8 was still a thrashing. This minor inaccuracy aside, the message was understood. "It's time," Kaveh Angoorani told the team. "It's our time."

Both Fremont and Riverside had "California" emblazoned

on their jerseys, not Northern or Southern California. Just "California."

"Who owns California?" Adams signed to his players again and again in the days before the game.

Like Army versus Navy or UCLA versus USC, the rivalry between the schools ran deep. Riverside staff said they could not help but notice that Fremonters, when referring to the Southern California school, seemed to sign "Riverside" derisively. The sign for "Riverside," which derives from the sign for *R*, is relatively simple, the index finger and the middle finger crossed, as if hoping for good luck. But Riversiders noticed that when Fremonters signed it, they held their hand low on their bodies, literally looking down on the school. In some cases, the crossed fingers were pointing toward the ground. It was a gesture that Coach Adams said was meant to resemble a drooping penis. "They are always up to dirty tricks," Adams complained in the days before the game.

The rivalry between the two schools seemed a natural extension of the enduring clash between Southern and Northern California, between palm trees and redwoods, between Los Angeles and San Francisco, between the Dodgers and the Giants, between Hollywood and Silicon Valley, between the oiled and tanned bodies of Kardashian culture and the notion, true or not, that with Stanford and Berkeley the north was necessarily more cerebral and less superficial.

Administrators, teachers, and coaches at the Fremont school would seldom miss an opportunity to point out that Fremont was the *original* California school for the deaf. The Fremont school saw itself as an integral part of America's deaf history, one of the earliest deaf institutions in the country. Its founding in San Francisco, after all, had preceded the chartering of Gallaudet University in Washington, the preeminent deaf learning institution in America, by four years. Riverside, by comparison, was an upstart, opening in 1953, nearly a century after its northern counterpart.

In football, Fremont had managed to maintain that sense of superiority. And they had the receipts to back it up. Riverside and Fremont had met forty-three times over five decades, with Fremont winning thirty-one times, more than two-thirds of their match-ups. More recently the results had been even more stark, as Coach Adams's spreadsheet, pasted to his players' lockers, made clear. The scores were permanently engraved onto a five-foot-tall trophy with a golden plaque that read THE BIG GAME. That trophy passed back and forth between the winners, but Fremont had been in possession of the trophy since 2009, a thirteen-year stretch of shame for Riverside. Although playing Fremont was traditionally an annual affair, a series of disasters, starting with wildfires and their smothering smoke, and then of course the pandemic, had canceled the 2017, 2018, 2019, and 2020 games. The 2021 game? Fremont had refused to play, infuriating the Riverside coaches. Fremont's head coach, Herminio Gonzalez, had prevaricated, despite an earlier agreement to play. They tried to hammer out details over FaceTime, but Gonzalez said the school's administration was not allowing him to go ahead with the game. Exasperated, Coach Adams gave up. "I said, 'You're just full of shit!' and hung up the phone." Gonzalez would later admit that they were reluctant to play because they judged their team weaker and they were afraid of losing to Riverside.

The tensions had carried over into the 2022 season, and in a measure of the intensity of the rivalry between the two schools, things got ugly. It's customary for high school coaches to exchange film of their past games with the teams they are about to meet. In that spirit, Coach Adams sent film of the Chadwick game to Herminio Gonzalez. But the film that Gonzalez posted in return was unwatchable, lasted only ten minutes, was out of focus, and was taken from odd angles. Gonzalez admitted it had been taken by a student. Fremont had also reached out to a Riverside rival, asking whether they would be interested in trying to get a Riverside player suspended because of an unsportsmanlike call in an earlier game. The gambit failed when the coach of the Riverside rival forwarded the text message to Coach Adams.

.   .   .

On a deceptively warm Saturday afternoon, all this intrigue, all this tension, would be replaced by a simpler question: Who was the better team? Or, as Coach Adams had again repeated to his players just before the game, "Who owns California?"

When the Cubs trotted onto the Fremont field, they saw some beefy opponents. Fremont had seven players over two hundred pounds. Ruben Guzman, who played both offensive and defensive line for Fremont, weighed in at nearly three hundred pounds, his girth stretching the numbers on his uniform. Johnte Haggins, their running back, was six feet tall and had the physique of someone who might be able to smash through a defensive line and leave bruises in his wake.

As each team assessed the other, stealing glances across the field, they had to remind themselves to be more guarded than usual. Both sides were so accustomed to playing hearing teams that players had gotten into the habit of openly using ASL. But here, against a deaf opponent, the coaches turned their bodies away from the field before signing to their players.

This was by no means the first time that deaf teams encountered the question of keeping their communication secret. More than a century earlier, the same dilemma had led to a significant contribution to the game of football: the invention of the huddle. Paul Hubbard, the quarterback for Gallaudet University in 1894, had faced a series of fellow deaf teams. His solution was to tell his teammates to meet before the play in a circle, backs toward any prying eyes. The huddle was born. Hubbard would later become an instructor at the Kansas State School for the Deaf, and he took his innovation with him. Hearing coaches took note, and the practice spread across the Midwest and then throughout the country. Today, Gallaudet celebrates the invention by selling T-shirts and other swag that read "Home of the Huddle."

Coach Adams's solution to the deaf-on-deaf dilemma was to make sure the entire playbook was encoded. He printed out a cheat sheet of two hundred plays, each with the corresponding codes. The players wore the list on their wrists, similar to how some NFL and college teams operate. Fremont had developed their own code system.

While games between hearing teams are preceded by the national anthem, Fremont tweaked the tradition to suit a deaf audience. The Fremont players in their orange-and-black uniforms turned toward the American flag flying beyond the end zone and formed a human chain, each player placing his hands on the shoulder pads of the player in front of him. Then a Fremont cheerleader took to the field and signed the words to the Pledge of Allegiance. The hearing referees stood at midfield, unsure of what was being signed but diligently facing the flag with their caps removed.

·   ·   ·

Fremont won the coin toss and would begin the Big Game rivalry receiving the ball.

As they did so often, the Cubs started with a squib kick that bounced eighteen yards and was momentarily fumbled by Fremont but recovered by the team's quarterback, Jaden Dingel, who, along with Fremont's starting running back, had been placed on the front lines during the kickoff. Fremont would start with decent field position, on their own thirty-one-yard line.

They kept the ball on the ground, and on the second play a wall of Fremont blockers opened a hole for Johnte Haggins to gain a first down. For a fleeting moment it looked like a promising start.

The campus of the California School for the Deaf, Riverside is dotted with palm trees. The San Gabriel Mountains loom in the background.

The Cubs were a small team, just two dozen players. They practiced and played their home games on the same field—rutted in places and with faded sideline paint.

Before home games the team had a ritual—a late lunch at a local pizzeria. They filled the place with red jerseys.

The Cubs' playing field was next to a busy four-lane road. Across the street was the Target parking lot where Phillip Castaneda slept in his father's car.

The Cubs' coaches had the advantage of being able to sign plays and instructions from the sidelines. Coach Keith Adams had encoded some of the plays so that even opponents who understood American Sign Language would not be able to intercept their play calls.

All eyes were on Coach Adams days before a big game against the Chadwick School. In the heat of the Riverside summer, the Cubs were relieved that Adams chose to give them a pep talk in the school's air-conditioned weight room.

Minutes from the California School for the Deaf, Riverside, acres of orange groves are reminders of the area's citrus legacy.

The school's five-decade-old scoreboard broke down before the start of the 2022 season. The athletic staff found a temporary replacement.

Kaveh Angoorani, the defensive coordinator, riled up the team before game time. He postponed his retirement so that he could stay with the team in their quest for a championship ring.

Trevin Adams was the heart and soul of the Cubs' offense. A quarterback who loved to run the ball, he was the very definition of a dual threat.

The California School for the Deaf had enough players for only a single football team. Freshmen, sophomores, and upperclassmen played together.

The invention of the iPhone was revolutionary for society—but for deaf students, and the Cubs in particular, it allowed students to stay in touch effortlessly day and night.

Trevin Adams shedding tackles and scoring a touchdown against Chadwick.

Jory Valencia, the leaping wide receiver, on the way to the championship game in 2022.

Supporters at the 2022 championship numbered in the hundreds, a far cry from the thousands who had turned out the year before.

The Cubs scouted their opponents at the 2022 championship. Felix Gonzales, their star receiver, kick returner, and all-around athlete, would watch from the sidelines, his shinbone shattered in a previous game.

Under the glare of the stadium lights, Gio Visco reached for a pass. With oversized hands, Visco was adept at the one-handed catch.

An ebullient Coach Adams during the 2022 championship.

The Cubs were well ahead at halftime in the championship, but Coach Adams urged his players not to let down their guard.

Jory Valencia celebrates a first down during the 2022 championship game.

In November 2021, the Los Angeles Chargers invited the Cubs to their stadium to watch a game against the Minnesota Vikings. The Cubs were introduced on the Jumbotron to a packed, cheering crowd.

Watching Cubs' games has been a rudimentary affair. After the *New York Times* article was published about the team, the administration of California governor Gavin Newsom vowed to build the school a stadium and new sports facilities.

But Riverside shut down the running lanes on the subsequent set of downs, and Fremont's drive stalled. They were forced to punt.

Back to receive was Felix Gonzales. The season was still young, this being the Cubs' third game, but Felix's name was lighting up the stat sheets. He had the most touchdowns, the most yards. He was closing in on two thousand total yards for his high school career, a Cubs record. On defense he was an instinctual safety, shutting down whatever receiver the coaches assigned him to. The defensive coaches liked to say they would just give Felix a jersey number and you could be almost certain that his opponent would not catch the ball. On special teams Felix was the kicker and the punter. And now he was back to receive, his sure-handedness and elusiveness filling the coaches with confidence.

But the punt sailed farther than Felix had calculated. From Fremont's twenty-yard line it flew all the way to the Cubs' nineteen-yard line. Felix backtracked to catch the ball and was immediately confronted with three Fremont players, unblocked and bearing down on him. They gang-tackled him, pushing him back seven yards as they slung him to the ground. Once back on his feet, Felix approached his teammate Luca Visco. "Why didn't you block?" he signed angrily.

A Fremont player then taunted Felix with his own commentary on the play. "You can't run," he signed to Felix. "You can't play." The trash talk had begun.

On their first offensive play of the game, the Cubs were spread wide, with two receivers on the right and their other receiver on the far left, a few paces from the left-hand sidelines. After a shotgun snap, Trevin faced the choice of handing it off to his brother, Kaden, or throwing a screen pass to Felix, who was waiting on the right wing, arms outstretched, ready to redeem himself from the disappointing kickoff return. True to form, Trevin chose a third option. He faked the handoff to his brother, ignored Felix, and tucked the ball close to his chest as he ran upfield, eluding a Fremont lineman, breaking free from another Fremont player who had grabbed a piece of his jersey, and barreling well past the first-down marker. From the spot where he had received his snap, on the ten-yard line, he ran twenty-seven yards before four Fremont players brought him down. On their first play from scrimmage, the Cubs had made a statement.

Sloppy procedural penalties by Fremont followed on the next three downs, putting the Cubs within striking distance of the end zone. The Cubs lined up wide again with Felix in the slot. The defense, showing their respect for the Cubs' speed, stood far off the line. Trevin received the snap, faked the handoff to Kaden, and threw a perfect pass over the middle that hit Felix, who had streaked past his defender, squarely in the chest. He darted into the end zone, leaving two Fremont players splayed on the turf. Felix trotted to the back of the end zone and signed to the Fremont fans lining the edge of the field. With the ball still in his left hand, he said, "Fremont is easy." More trash talk.

The Cubs lined up for a two-point conversion. Felix ran a route that had him streaming left toward the middle and then juking sharply rightward toward the sidelines. His speed left the defense in disarray, and he caught an easy pass in the end zone. The Fremont cornerback he had burned on the last play got burned again, left only to watch the catch three paces behind.

On the sidelines, Michael Mabashov, the Cubs' assistant coach, was greeting his players excitedly, signing repeatedly, "More of that!"

Fremont found momentum on their next drive, and for a moment it looked as if it could be an evenly matched game. But the drive stopped there with a whump. Trevin Adams shot through a gap in the line and pile-drived Irving Senegal, a 163-pound running back, into the ground. The hit looked almost circus-like, with Trevin launching himself at the running back as if springing himself from a high dive, Trevin's shoulder plowing into the Fremont player and his feet dangling in the air like some made-for-television wrestling move. One failed pass and another stuffed run later, Fremont handed the ball back to Riverside on downs.

At times the Cubs looked far from invincible. Jory Valencia bobbled and dropped a well-thrown pass, and another pass, one that if caught looked certain to result in a touchdown, drifted just beyond his fingertips. But they eventually found their groove. They drove down the field, mixing their runs and passes. At the school where their parents met, Trevin got the snap, took two steps, and then flipped the ball back to Kaden, who made it to the two-yard line. The Riverside brothers were teaming up to bulldoze their parental alma mater. One successful drive followed the next. It was 24–0 at halftime, and there seemed little question who would win the battle for California. By the end of the third quarter, it was 46–0. The final score: 54–6.

After shaking hands with the Fremont players, the Cubs gathered on the field and posed for pictures with their prize, the five-foot-tall BIG GAME trophy. The next day they would pack it into a van on its way to the glass cases at the entrance to the Riverside athletic facility.

25

Playing a Deaf Legend

U p next for the Cubs, one week later, was the game against
the Indiana School for the Deaf, a team led by a sixty-five-
year-old head coach well known in the deaf community, Michael
Paulone. The Deaf Hoosiers, as the Indiana team was called, were
4-0, and a lot of the credit flowed to Paulone, who had coached
high school football for three decades.

That Paulone had a winning team was a notable achievement
given the size of the Indiana school. There were only fifty boys in
the high school, so he took what he could get. They had not had a
losing season in a decade. Even more impressive was that the team
played eleven-man ball. In Riverside, the Indiana team would have
to adjust to the speed and agility of the eight-man game.

Deaf from birth, Paulone had not let that get in the way of competing in the hearing world of high school football in his home-
town of Philadelphia. Growing up in an Italian immigrant family,
Paulone attended the Pennsylvania School for the Deaf and shone
as a quarterback there.

Philadelphia holds an annual all-star game, public schools versus private schools, showcasing the hundred athletes judged the
best in the city. In 1977, Paulone was selected as one of four quar-

terbacks representing the private schools. It was a huge honor. But he ran into a mental roadblock, not in *his* head, but in those of the hearing coaches, who were skeptical that they could deal with a deaf quarterback. How would he communicate with the rest of the team? How would he tell the wide receivers and linemen the next play in the huddle? Paulone was relegated to the fourth string, a deeply frustrating outcome for a talented and ambitious student athlete. He came up with a plan. Paulone persuaded his coach from the deaf school, Bob Stein, to help with communication. Stein, who was hearing but knew ASL, devised a system where he would get the play from the head coach and then sign it to Paulone on the field. It was then up to a running back to deliver the instructions to the other players in the huddle. It was a simple and elegant solution that allowed Paulone to move from fourth string to third, to second, and then finally Michael Paulone, the deaf kid on an all-hearing team, got the job he had deserved all along. He became the starting quarterback.

Formally known as the Philadelphia City All-Star Football Game, the event was attended by dozens of college scouts among the 13,400 spectators. Paulone played the first quarter and then was rotated out to allow the other quarterbacks to play. When the fourth quarter came around, his team was down 8–0. The coaches put Paulone back in the game. He rallied down the field, completing five straight passes. A columnist watching the game noted that three hundred supporters from the Pennsylvania School for the Deaf, PSD for short, cheered from the stands. "With every completion, the 600 hands attached to the 300 students from PSD waggled excitedly, a symphony of silence accompanying the boisterous cheering in the rest of the stands."

Paulone's fifth completion was a dart, a seventeen-yard touchdown into a strong wind. He followed that with another pass into the end zone for the two-point conversion. The game was well covered in the local press, and the player who made the two-

point catch, Gerry Smith, was quoted in the papers the next day.
"I thought that Mike's not being able to talk would be too much
of a handicap to overcome," Smith said. "But he's got those eyes,
there's something about the way he looks at you. It's like he's saying, 'Come on, have confidence in me, I'll take us somewhere.' And
boy, he did."

The game ended in a tie, 8–8, but for Paulone it was almost
as good as a victory. He was named Most Valuable Player for the
private school all-star team and awarded the trophy by Dick Vermeil, the legendary coach of the Philadelphia Eagles. Paulone
would then serve as ball boy for the Eagles for five years, traveling the country with the team. Vermeil said in a 2022 interview
that he had a tradition of allowing his coaches to bring in one
young player, usually a son, to help out with tasks on the field and
in the locker room. His sons too old for the job, Vermeil took in
Paulone.

On a trip to Los Angeles, Paulone and a friend, a fellow ball
boy, snuck into the locker room of the Eagles' opponents, the
Rams. They were hoping to spot their boyhood hero, Joe Namath,
who had grown up in Pennsylvania and was playing his final season in the NFL after his illustrious career with the Jets, including
the Super Bowl victory in 1969 against the Baltimore Colts. The
two young men tracked down Namath and introduced themselves.
"Michael Paulone?" Namath said. "You are the deaf kid who
played quarterback for the all-star team in Philadelphia." It was
a moment that Paulone would recount decades later, a smile from
ear to ear, still awed with the wonder of the encounter.

·   ·   ·

In Riverside, hours before the game against the Cubs, Paulone was
braced for a tough game. He had seen the Cubs' film and had followed their playoff run a year earlier. But he promised to bring a

high level of physicality. He used an oceanic analogy: Riverside, he said, might be a shark. But his Deaf Hoosiers were dolphins. "People think that if a dolphin fights a shark, then the shark will win," Paulone said. "But the dolphin knows where to hit." And with that he pointed to his chest. "Hitting is our team's strength," he said. "We stay tough, we play physical, we play to the fourth quarter."

His words would prove partly true. Yes, the game was physical, as Paulone wanted it, but it was never close.

On offense and defense, the Cubs dominated. They sacked Indiana ten times. Through a balanced game of runs and passes they had fourteen first downs, compared with just four for Indiana. They completely shut down Indiana's running game, keeping the Deaf Hoosiers to a net of just three yards on the ground for the entire game. The final score was 62–18.

Even in their weaker moments the Cubs were dominant, something made abundantly clear by a play early in the second quarter. The Cubs were nine yards away from scoring their third unanswered touchdown of the game. Trevin Adams stood in the shotgun ready to receive the snap. Next to him was Cody Metzner, the Mack truck of a running back. The ball was badly snapped and landed on the grass in front of Trevin. Instead of quickly scooping it up, he inadvertently swatted the ball to his right and then found himself bent over like a farm boy chasing a chicken. When he finally got hold of the football and looked upfield, Cody had single-handedly and simultaneously knocked two Indiana players out of his way. Felix had blocked the left-side linebacker. Only one Indiana defensive player stood between Trevin and the goal line, Jayden DeFalco, a six-foot, 168-pound safety, who was also the team's talented quarterback. Trevin lowered his shoulder in a way that recalled some 1930s poster of a football player in a leather helmet, and the two boys met with a thud, shoulder to shoulder. Trevin smashed across the goal line with his momentum and landed victoriously in the end zone. DeFalco, resentful at being bulldozed and pancaked, stood up and shoved Adams on his way back to the sidelines. For DeFalco and his team, the depressing message had been received: even on a busted play, the Cubs could manhandle them.

It was the Cubs who played the game to the fourth quarter, never letting up, even with their huge lead, and keeping in the starting lineup well into the second half. By the third quarter the Indiana girls' volleyball team, which had also competed that day in Riverside and was on the sidelines, stopped paying attention to the game. At 62–18, it was an embarrassing loss for Paulone, and it seemed to wound his pride.

"They were the better team," Paulone said after the game, "in everything."

Referring to the blowout, he added bitterly, "I think their coach can do a better job of having more class."

.   .   .

By the time the Cubs were preparing for their final deaf opponent of the season, the Florida School for the Deaf and the Blind, the coaches were discussing not whether they would win but by how much. Coach Adams wanted decisive victories so there would be no question that they were the national deaf champions.

The day before the game, a repairman came to the Cubs' field to fix the scoreboard, which was half a century old and had stopped working before the season was under way. The repairman replaced the two-digit digital display that showed the home team's score. This led to jokes that given the lopsided scores in the Cubs' victories, maybe he should have installed three digits so the team wouldn't be limited to ninety-nine points. By the end of the Florida game, this wasn't a joke anymore.

Just before the game, Eric LeFors, the Florida head coach, had smiled outside the locker room where his players were suiting up, setting aside any pregame bravado. "I hope we get some points," LeFors said.

The Florida team did indeed come away with points, but just barely. The final score was 84–8. The Cubs had been sixteen points away from needing to worry about the two-digit scoreboard.

What came after the final whistle was in some ways more instructive than the game itself, and a reflection of the Cubs' total dominance. A number of deaf commentators on social media lashed out at Riverside for not showing mercy.

An administrator at the California School for the Deaf in Fremont said it was "not necessary to run up high scores" and called it bad sportsmanship.

An alumnus of the Maryland School for the Deaf, a football powerhouse in its own right, was even more cutting. "What are you teaching these children, really?" the commenter asked. "You're creating an intimidating, toxic masculinity culture that thrives on fear."

Two weeks earlier Maryland had beat Florida 66–0, so the criticism seemed misplaced. But there *was* something that evoked pity when a one-sided win reached into the 80s. A year earlier a similar outcry had ensued after a school in the Los Angeles area, Inglewood High School, beat its rival, Morningside, 106–0. The spat between those two hearing teams had resulted in the Inglewood principal apologizing. "We did not conduct ourselves with sportsmanship and integrity and the final score was unacceptable," the principal said. Inglewood had refused to run the clock in the fourth quarter; California has what is called a mercy rule, allowing for time to run down without stoppages between plays in the fourth quarter if one team is winning by more than thirty-five points.

In the Cubs' game against Florida, the mercy rule *had* been put into effect. Without it, the score might well have been in the triple digits.

Within a few weeks the criticism that the Cubs and Coach Adams had received online petered out. Adams, in any case, had never batted an eye.

"I can't let other people control me and get in my head," he said. "I have to do what's in the best interest of my team."

The lopsided victories had certainly mattered to the algorithm that ranks teams in California, the key measurement used by league officials in selecting schools for the playoffs. With a record of 5-0, the Cubs were now ranked second among the 105 varsity teams in California playing eight-man football.

26

Felix

Felix Gonzales was having a standout game. As always. Against Calvary Chapel, a Christian school a dozen miles south of downtown Los Angeles, the Cubs were dominating and Felix was a big reason why. A screen pass up the right-hand sideline for fifteen yards. A handoff and a dash for thirty yards down the other side-line. By far the fastest player on the Cubs, Felix was living up to the nickname his teammates had given him: the Cheetah. Then came a fifty-five-yard punt return, where he outran all but three Calvary players, and when confronted at the two-yard line by those last three Calvary Chapel defensemen, he writhed his way out of a leg tackle, acrobatically arched backward, and, almost as if perform-ing a trust fall, held the ball over his head and crashed into the end zone, face toward the sky. This elegant feat of athleticism would have been a touchdown had the line judge not mistakenly believed that Felix had stepped out of bounds at the thirty-yard line. (He had not, as was later clear on the game tape.) Never mind, Felix thought to himself. I'll just wait for the next chance. Two plays later it came. Positioned as the slot receiver, he gunned off the line, streaked past the safeties who were double-teaming him, and reached down to his knees to catch an underthrown pass in the end zone. He then casually flipped the football to the referee who, two plays earlier, had made the wrong call on the punt return. No hard feelings.

These were among the last plays Felix Gonzales would ever make for the California School for the Deaf, Riverside football team.

His very last play would come early in the second quarter. Felix stood on the line of scrimmage, craning his head left to the sidelines, where Coach Adams signed the play to the team: 12 Bubble. The play meant he would be getting the ball quickly, as soon as Trevin Adams could throw it to him. But when the snap came, it was low, nearly hitting the ground and forcing Trevin to crouch down to grab it. In the time it took for Trevin to get the pass off, Felix was already looking back, eager to receive the ball. It's often said that football is a game of inches. It's also a game of split seconds. Enough time in the play had been lost for the Calvary defensive back to read it and sprint toward the line. Trevin's pass was slightly long, and it brushed off Felix's fingers just as the defensive back came crashing into him.

It was an awkward collision that looked out of place in a football game, as if two office workers sprinting down a Manhattan sidewalk to catch a bus had smacked into each other. Both players were upright on impact. You almost expected the defensive back to mutter, "Excuse me, sir," and go on his way. But some part of the defensive player's body—maybe a knee, maybe the tip of a shoe—had struck Felix hard.

After impact, he fell toward the turf strangely contorted. He took a halting step, put his hands forward, and landed on his knees, bracing for the ground. Facedown, he slowly turned his body and reached for his left leg.

Weeks later, with the shooting pains of the injury still haunting him, Felix would piece together what had happened. Oddly, he said, there was a lot he did not remember about the game, as if the trauma of the day had been an eraser on the whiteboard of his memory, selectively rubbing out large chunks of the game.

He remembers seeing Trevin throwing the ball to him, the ball falling away, and then closing his eyes to brace for the slam of the defensive player bearing down on him. The first pain he experienced was in his chest. "My heart hurt," he said. "I literally felt my heart squeeze really hard." Then he felt the intense pain coming from his left leg.

As he lay on the turf, he remembered seeing Jory, his fellow wide receiver, and he recalled signing to Jory, "I'm out, I'm done."

He did not remember Galvin Drake approaching him on the field.

"It's just a minor injury; you deal with this all the time," Galvin signed to Felix. "Don't worry about it. You're going to be fine. It's just a bruise."

Galvin had seen Felix take hits and deliver hits, and he knew Felix was not a whiner. Felix had a high threshold for pain and an ability to play through it.

But now, as he gazed at Felix on the ground, Galvin started to have doubts about this injury. Felix's face had blanched, and his facial contortions suggested he was in agony. When Felix tried to get up and stand on his own, he faltered. Felix looked at Galvin and signed, "I can't."

He put all his weight on Galvin as they moved slowly off the field. Once on the sidelines he lay on the ground, surrounded by concerned teammates.

In the bleachers above, Felix's mother, Delia, was talking with her old classmates. She was a graduate of CSDR, and football games served as mini alumni reunions. A friend interrupted her conversation, pointing to the scrum of players, and told her that it was Felix they were all gathered around. She ran down the steps, rushing with maternal adrenaline and fear. Felix's hands were shaking; his legs were trembling. As she looked more closely, she saw that her son's whole body was quivering. She was scared. Tears were flowing down her son's cheeks. A medical trainer told her and the coaches there was a 99 percent chance Felix had broken a bone and recommended that they take him to an emergency room. They crammed him into the back bench of the family pickup truck, Felix's left leg swelling up.

As they left for the hospital, they were also leaving behind the deaf world. The ease of the sign-language conversations that Delia had been enjoying with other deaf parents in the stands would soon be replaced by the language barrier that the deaf community encounters whenever they step into hearing settings. Delia and her son would ultimately go to five hospitals; some medical staff would tell her that they did not accept her Medicaid insurance. One hospital said they did not have the materials to make a cast. All but one doctor told Felix he needed surgery. The last doctor they saw said it would heal in a cast. Delia communicated with medical staff by scribbling on a piece of paper. The American medical system and all its associated complications of insurance, paperwork, and general confusion can be an ordeal for the most determined hearing people. It was a nightmare for a deaf mother and son.

The staff at the first hospital they visited told Felix he would need to remove his football pants for the X-ray. Felix had no idea how he would roll off the skintight football uniform. Given the urgent circumstances, he showed a remarkable respect for the school's equipment: he texted Coach Adams and asked permission to cut off the pants. Adams quickly assented, and Felix was off to the X-ray room.

In medical lingo, the image that came up showed a mid-shaft tibia fracture. In the language of everyone else, Felix's shinbone looked as if someone had taken a chisel and hammered it in half. It was an unusual football injury. Ankle sprains, shoulder dislocations, mangled fingers, busted knee ligaments—these were common to the game of football. A shin cracked in two? Emergency rooms dealt with these after bad car crashes, not high school football games. Felix left the hospital with a bunch of ACE bandages and the knowledge that he was only beginning a long medical journey.

.   .   .

The players had continued their rout of their opponents after Felix was carried away. At halftime the Cubs' lead was 54–0. But no one saw this as a triumph. The Calvary Chapel Grizzlies were in the bottom half of the statewide rankings; there had never been a doubt in the minds of the Riverside coaches and players that the Cubs would win. The score hardly mattered. Even before the game, the Cubs had clinched their place in the playoffs.

In the locker room at halftime word spread that it was very likely that Felix might be out for the season. Coach Adams called for two minutes of silence. In a deaf context, this meant heads bowed and lights dimmed as the stunned players grappled with the sudden loss of their star player.

Trevin began weeping. He blamed himself for throwing the pass late and putting Felix in a vulnerable position. Teammates gathered around their quarterback, trying to comfort him. With tears flowing and downcast eyes all around, the locker room began to feel like the reception hall of a funeral home. There was no comfort in knowing that they had lost Felix on a meaningless play in a meaningless game.

The Cubs ultimately won the game 66–6. But as the team bus pulled away from this Pyrrhic victory, phones began to vibrate with a text message. It was the X-ray of Felix's tibia, an image that brought a strangely sudden finality to it all. They saw for themselves the bone cracked in half.

Galvin, the assistant coach, grappled with the meaning of what had happened. "Felix loves football," he said. "He's a senior and I don't know if he's going to play college football. It's possible that this could be the last game of his life."

Galvin saw it as a moment of reflection, not just for Felix. "It really made our players get chills. I told them to take every moment as seriously as possible because you don't know when it could be your turn to have that last game of your life. Cherish your time here and play as hard as you can, practice as hard as you can."

.   .   .

With a cast that extended almost to his hip, Felix recuperated at home south of Los Angeles.

He spent most of his time lying in bed, the least distressing position for his leg. He took prescribed pills to alleviate shooting pains. But the pills also made him feel dizzy.

Being home reminded him of what he called the "COVID doom," the solitary months that he had spent in lockdowns during the early stages of the pandemic. The loneliness made him feel reflective. "I realize how much I need people and how much I need football," he said from the brown couch of his family's small, crowded living room. He thought about what came next, what he would do after graduating in the spring. Maybe work at Amazon. Or maybe get a job in a barbershop. His brother had taught him how to cut hair. He would take a year off, earn some money, and then go to a community college and play football again.

He watched the replay of his injury over and over and over again, wishing the play had never happened. One lousy play had changed his life.

"In that very moment someone put a pin in the balloon of my dreams," he said.

Just before the Calvary Chapel game, Trevin had taken him aside. "Congratulations, you are about to hit two thousand yards." Felix hadn't been aware of this impending milestone. Trevin told him he was only 119 yards short of 2,000 receiving yards for his high school years, a remarkable number given that Felix's sophomore football season had been canceled because of the pandemic. After the injury he was still a few dozen yards short. He asked the doctor treating his broken leg whether he could go back into a game just for one play. That's all he would need to get to the 2,000 mark. Not surprisingly, the doctor said no.

His team had sent him a poster with handwritten get-well messages from each player. And they recorded a short video. Felix watched it: Jory stood in the first row of a semicircle of players. The video was filmed in Coach Adams's classroom under the glow of fluorescent bulbs. Players in the back rows stood on chairs. Everyone looked into the camera. "I know that we have unfinished business," Jory said, referring to the championship that they were all so hungry to capture. "We are going to win it, Felix. For you." The video made him choke up.

The Cubs had lost their fastest player, their most versatile player, who was simply listed as "athlete" on the depth chart. One of the coaches had flatteringly compared Felix to Troy Polamalu, the Steelers' strong safety who was called the Tasmanian Devil because he seemed to be everywhere on the field—explosively. Felix was, in the words of Laura Edwards, the head of athletics at the school, the team's difference maker. Questions churned in everyone's mind. How would the team fare without him?

On the night of Felix's injury, Coach Adams awoke at 4:00 a.m., his head filled with panicked thoughts. Should he change the playbook now that their playmaker was gone? Did they still have a chance at the championship?

At practice on Monday, with the team still in shock, Adams gathered the players.

"We won't be able to execute these great big showstopping plays like before. But we can still do our job," Coach Adams told them. "We can keep going. You guys need to step up.

"This is not a one-man show," the coach told his players. "We only need eight men to get to that championship game."

27

The Speech

Even as the team was reeling from Felix's injury, spirits were lifted by the computations of a computer algorithm. After taking into account the scores of the weekend's games, including the Cubs' 66–6 victory over Calvary Chapel, the California School for the Deaf, Riverside had shot to first place among the 105 teams that play eight-man ball in California. No deaf team in the state had ever reached first place on the list before. The official ranking, published by an organization called CalPreps, is generated automatically, taking into account the strength of a team's opponents and margins of victories. The ranking gave the Cubs more than just prestige. The CalPreps score is used to determine which teams make the playoffs. Even with three games to go in the regular season, the Cubs were assured a spot. And if they manhandled their opponents the way they had so far, they were likely to be the No. 1 seed. It went without saying that this ranking went only so far. A computer decided this; championship seasons are won on the field, not by an algorithm.

The Cubs' next game was against United Christian Academy, a school in Rancho Cucamonga, a half-hour drive from Riverside at the foot of the San Gabriel Mountains. Before the game, Coach

Adams was once again contacted by the NFL. Could they film him giving his pregame speech again? The NFL producers had not been satisfied with Keith's speech in the Chadwick game, when Kurt Warner had visited, so they wanted to do a second take. Always obliging, Adams said yes. He came up with a short speech and sent it to them:

> For the first time in history, we are ranked number 1 in the state. So let's go out and show we are number 1!
>
> They hate the idea of losing to a deaf team so let's kick their butts. Let's take some names like we did all this season!
>
> Felix is not playing tonight. He gave everything for this team and he wants us to play even harder without him. Let's do this for Felix.
>
> Let's go out there and play with fire!

The NFL producers responded with an entirely remade speech. They kept some of the same themes but gave the speech more of a cadence. They sent Coach Adams this revised version, which the team's interpreter, Mark Bayarsky, would read as Adams signed it to the team:

> They are bigger, they are stronger, but they don't know what we have in our hearts!
>
> They think because we're deaf we can't compete, but they don't know what we have in our hearts!
>
> They think that because one of our best players is out, they have an advantage, but they don't know what we have in our hearts!
>
> For the first time in history, we are ranked number 1 in the state. . . . They think it won't last. They think we will fail. . . . But they don't know what we have in our hearts!
> NOW LET'S GO OUT AND SHOW THEM!!!!!

The NFL version had one flourish that seemed to strain the truth slightly. The Cubs might have been smaller than some of their opponents, but they had proven that they were often physically stronger. This was certainly the verdict of the coaches and players on opposing teams. Before the game with the United Christian Academy Eagles, Xavier Forte, the team's head coach, said he was expecting such a hard-hitting performance by the Cubs that he had told his players that they might require an ice bath at the end of it, and a weekend of recovery.

"It's one of those games where you have to buckle up both of your chin straps," Forte said before the game. "You're probably not going to be doing anything Saturday."

Forte lauded the Cubs' physicality. "They're nasty," he said, meaning it as a compliment. "I love it personally because it makes you have to step up. There are certain games you can get away with being the faster team or the more athletic team or the more talented team. But there are certain times where you have to buckle up and play football. And at the end of the day that's what they make you do."

The Cubs filed into the locker room at Rancho Cucamonga before the game, trailed by the NFL cameraman wearing the same rig with the pulleys and levers that looked like an exoskeleton. In their clean white uniforms and scarlet pants, the players sat in two orderly rows, awaiting instructions from both their coaches and the NFL producers.

"Do you want me to leave the hat on or take it off?" Coach Adams asked the NFL crew. Adams, like the rest of the coaching staff, was neatly dressed in a red polo shirt, black Nike shorts, and a black baseball cap. "Pull it off," the cameraman said after a brief assessment. He choreographed the shot, making players scoot back and forth and leaving a center aisle for Coach Adams to walk up and down, creating the perfect locker-room scene that viewers around the country would see on their screens.

The cameraman gave the signal, and Coach Adams began signing the speech. Bayarsky, the interpreter, read the scripted words
from the piece of paper he had been given by the NFL. When
Bayarsky got to the line about the team being No. 1 in the state
for the first time in history, the players jumped to their feet
enthusiastically.

But the speech wasn't supposed to be over just yet. So the NFL
producers asked Adams to do it again. With game time nearing,
and after the second take, the players filed out onto the field.

.   .   .

The job of replacing Felix largely fell to a freshman and a sophomore, both with the last name Visco. They were cousins from a large
deaf-hearing family with Italian roots that had settled in Pennsylvania and California. Gio Visco, the freshman, was five feet, nine
inches, a natural athlete who had trouble getting footwear because
of his size 13 feet. He also had oversized hands that required XXL
gloves, big mitts that he used to pluck balls one-handedly from the
sky. He had done this in the game against the Florida School for the
Deaf and the Blind, drawing gasps and cheers from the sidelines.
He played wide receiver and defensive back, but he had a strong
arm and could sub in as quarterback, too, a position he had played
in middle school.

Gio had played basketball on hearing teams when he was
younger and shared the sentiments of his deaf friends: feeling isolated, his talents wasted. "They wouldn't include me, and I didn't
know what I was supposed to do," Gio said. The experience had
given him a sense of mission. "We are trying to prove everybody
wrong," he said about playing on the Cubs. "Just because I sign
and you hear, that doesn't make a difference in our athletic ability."

Gio had looked up to Felix as a mentor on the team, quizzing
him on how he could increase his speed, improve his footwork.

Felix had advised him on weight-lifting techniques that could strengthen his leg muscles. After Felix's injury, Gio took a Sharpie to the back plate of his football pads. "We are doing this for Felix," he wrote on the pads, which would stick out from the back of his jersey during practice.

Luca Visco, his cousin, was five feet, ten inches tall and had the same lean athleticism. He was one of only two African Americans on the team. His mother, who died when he was young, had been born in Ethiopia, and Luca was vice president of the Black student club on campus, a small group in a school that was overwhelmingly Latino and white.

Headstrong and confident, Luca had frustrated coaches with what they described as an I-know-best attitude. Michael Mabashov, the assistant coach charged with defensive backs, told Luca his footwork was lazy. It caused him to miss some big plays. This issue came to the fore early in the game against the United Christian Academy Eagles. Luca had allowed the Eagles' wide receiver to blaze past him, catch an easy pass, and jog for a touchdown. The play seemed to raise questions about the Cubs' chances in the play-offs. Were Felix's replacements, an untested freshman and sophomore, not up to the task?

The fears were quickly allayed in the game against the Eagles, a matchup that the Cubs were quite confident of winning. The Visco cousins found a higher gear. Gio Visco caught a kickoff at his own ten-yard line and ran it back, zigzagging from one sideline to the other, for an improbable touchdown. Seven Eagles players missed their tackles. One member of the Eagles' kickoff team, a six-foot, 170-pound lineman, dove for Gio Visco's legs but couldn't hold on and was flung to the turf. He picked himself up, ran downfield, caught up with Gio Visco zagging back across the field, and missed again. There were two ways of looking at this play. Terrible tackling or great running. It was a combination of both.

Luca would shine, too. Late in the second quarter, with the

Cubs on defense, he cut in front of an Eagles receiver, intercepted a pass, and ran the ball back for forty-five yards. A few drives later, he did it again. The game was a festival of intercepted passes by the Cubs. Gio Visco also had one, and Trevin Adams ran one back for a touchdown. Altogether the Cubs had six interceptions in the game.

Just before halftime the game was all but decided, with the Cubs ahead 42–6. But the Cubs wanted more. On the Eagles' final drive before the half, Kaveh Angoorani called a time-out to preserve the final seconds for a possible offensive drive. "Isn't forty-two points enough?" one of the referees said to no one in particular. The same referee, later in the game, would remark admiringly about the Cubs, "These guys don't drop passes."

When the team had gathered in the locker room at halftime, Coach Adams announced that many first-stringers would not be playing the second half. Cody Metzner, the team's tackling and blocking dynamo, had to be carried to the locker room because of a leg injury. It turned out to just be a bad bruise. But the coaches were already spooked by Felix's injury and didn't want to risk any more starters going down.

As the coaches were announcing other adjustments for the second half, the NFL cameraman showed his phone to Coach Adams with a message he had typed. Could they redo the last part of the pregame speech? Adams agreed and the players and coaches, some with barely concealed expressions of disbelief on their faces, took their positions again. Keith looked down at a copy of the speech he had on the locker-room bench and, with remarkable conjured enthusiasm, delivered the phrases again that the NFL had prepared for him. This time the camera was behind him. The coaches and players then spilled out into the concrete hallways of the athletic facility on their way back onto the field. Kaveh Angoorani couldn't hold it in anymore. He laughed and shook his head. The spectacle was over. It was time to play football again.

Down by thirty-six points, the coaches of United Christian

Academy asked to run the clock continuously for the second half. For the Cubs players who normally sat on the bench, the second half was a rare chance to show their stuff. They came away with moments that they would probably play and replay in their minds' eyes for a lifetime.

Salvador Cruz, a five-foot, seven-inch, 240-pound sophomore who was still learning the ropes on the defensive line, was sent in for the last defensive series of the game. At practices he was affable and exceedingly polite. He took it upon himself to remind his teammates to pay attention during team meetings and film sessions. If there was such a thing as seeming too nice for football, Sal demonstrated it. He grew up in the Central Valley, outside Bakersfield, a two-and-a-half-hour drive from Riverside. His mother was deaf and his father hearing, both of them of Mexican heritage. His mother packed boxes at a warehouse, and his father was a mechanic. Sal's dream was to own a farm like the one his uncle had when he was growing up. He had picked grapes for his uncle's small winery. Now living in the dormitories at CSDR, he saw his family on weekends. When the coaches put him into the game against the Eagles, Sal was playing left defensive end across from a good-sized offensive lineman. On his second play at the line, he wrestled his way around the lineman and found himself two short steps away from the quarterback, who was trying to extract himself from the pocket. Sal grabbed the quarterback by his shoulder pads and pulled him down. The Cubs' sidelines roared with approval at the sight of their rookie teammate's sack. Christian Jimenez ran from his linebacker position to congratulate him. On the bus ride back to his parents' home that evening, the clip of his tackle became available online, and he sent it to his parents. When he got home, they all went out for some Texas barbecue to celebrate.

For Joshua Cypert, a diminutive junior, the game against the Eagles risked being a disaster. Cypert, a carpenter's son from Los Angeles with Cherokee, German, and Filipino heritage, had been put in as a cornerback and was outrun by an Eagles wide receiver for their second touchdown. It was a play that might have lived in his nightmares for years: a rare opportunity for field time, and he had blown it. But by the time the final play of the game came around, Cypert was still in the game. The Eagles sent their receivers deep, and the quarterback rolled out right and heaved the ball to the center of the field. Cypert undercut the receiver, caught the ball, and ran it back ten yards before being tackled as the game clock ran out. The Cubs' sidelines swarmed toward Cypert to congratulate him, jumping up and down with joy. Cypert beamed. When both teams lined up to shake hands at midfield, Cypert took his place in line, still clinging to his intercepted ball.

28

"I'm Playing! I'm Playing!"

Sometimes a team's biggest opponent isn't on the field. As the playoffs approached and eight squads of eager high school boys prepared to vie for Southern California's eight-man football championships, the Cubs were challenged by a microscopic foe.

Jory Valencia couldn't understand why he was so exhausted. His parents knew him to be stoic, rarely complaining about ailments. But for a week, the Cubs' leading wide receiver had been laid low. He was sleeping more than usual. During practices, when he tried to run, it was painful, and he found it hard to breathe. He complained of headaches, too. "He has a very high pain tolerance," said Jory's dad, Jeremias Valencia, who was one year into his job as the school's athletic director. "When he said he was in pain, I knew it was serious."

Two days before the playoffs began, Jory's parents took him to urgent care, where a doctor diagnosed walking pneumonia. Pneumonia, an infection of the air sacs in the lungs, can be mild or life-threatening, depending on the severity and on the patient's age and health. Walking pneumonia is an informal term for the milder variety, treatable with antibiotics and rest. Jory went home with strict instructions from the doctor: No strenuous activity for seven days. No school for ten days.

The Cubs had lost Felix, their No. 1 wide receiver and defensive back. Now they were stunned to learn that they would be entering the playoffs without Jory, their standout receiver and team leader in interceptions. Jory had developed a strong ability to read quarterbacks, a skill that the younger players who would step up to take his place were only starting to grasp.

The Cubs had breezed through the end of their regular season and had been getting antsy. They had a bye, and then their last scheduled game never happened: a Lutheran school in Los Angeles County had forfeited four days before they were scheduled to play the Cubs. The Lutheran school's athletic director sent a terse email saying that injuries had left them "without enough players to field our team."

Now, in the first round of the playoffs, the Cubs were the No. 1 seed. They were three games away from a possible rematch with Faith Baptist, the No. 2 seed and also undefeated. They were looking at three more games. Quarterfinal, semifinal, championship.

In the quarterfinals, the Cubs were facing the Leadership Military Academy Wolfpack, a team they had played early in the season. In that game, the Wolfpack had given the Cubs a scare. On a hot day in early September, the Wolfpack had been within two points of taking the lead at halftime. The Cubs' thin lead was 26–24, and it had made them nervous. In the second half, the Cubs had made adjustments and shut down the Wolfpack, winning the game 54–26. But that was with a healthy Cubs team with their receiving corps intact. The rematch would be without Felix or Jory, their most sure-handed players.

The Wolfpack prided themselves on being tough kids. Leadership Military Academy is a charter school in Moreno Valley, a half-hour drive from Riverside, and run by a Brooklyn-born ex-marine, Santos Campos. The students are required to wear uniforms and boots and have morning meetings in military formation, presided over by another ex-marine, a former drill sergeant. Most students at the academy are from low-income families, and 80 percent meet the state's requirements to qualify for free or reduced lunches. Some come to the school because of disciplinary problems elsewhere. Others, like J'wan Wilson, a muscular six-foot, one-inch senior, chose the school because he saw his life headed in the wrong direction. After attending the local large public high school his freshman year, Wilson said he had assessed his chances of a good education. "I was around bad people, and I wasn't staying in my classes," he said. He transferred to Leadership Military Academy. With 150 students in grades nine through twelve, the academy was small enough to be flexible with students and to talk through their challenges. Many students had after-school jobs at the nearby warehouses that were paying $19 an hour, money they needed to supplement their family's budget. The previous year, Wilson had worked at Jack in the Box, the burger chain, for $16.50 an hour. This year he was interviewing for a job at one of Amazon's warehouses. He juggled classwork, football practices, and his after-school job.

On the field, Wilson was the team's biggest threat, a physical linebacker who loved making big hits. On offense he played running back. "The ability to run and hit people. That's my favorite thing about football," he said a few days before the game against the Cubs.

. . .

On game day at home, the Cubs' roster filed into the locker room shadowed by their coaches in their matching black tracksuits and hoodies. Then a surprise appearance: Jory Valencia, the walking pneumonia patient. He had convinced his father and the coaches that he could play. "I knew if I missed the game, my high school career could be over," he said. He looked like a ghost, his sunken eyes rimmed by black circles, his bony face more gaunt than usual. Jory had slept badly the night before. He felt nauseated. He was not his jovial self. But he had greeted his family that morning with a mantra. "I'm playing! I'm playing! I'm playing!"

His father was skeptical.

"He looked terrible, so I said, 'We'll see. We'll see.'"

As he arrived at the locker room, Jory approached Kaveh Angoorani and gave him a hug. In the middle of the embrace Kaveh wondered to himself if he would contract pneumonia from this close contact. When he thought about it later, he calculated that it was worth the risk. "If it's a choice between pneumonia and winning the championship, I'll take pneumonia," Kaveh said. "Pneumonia is only temporary. Winning is forever."

The coaches discussed a number of ways they could deploy Jory. Jeremias suggested that if Jory didn't feel well enough, he could come in as a sort of decoy, playing the first few snaps so that the Wolfpack had no inkling he was sick.

Right until game time Jory didn't know how he would fare.

"I know my limits. We'll see what happens. The most important thing is to win the game," he said.

Coach Adams sent the team onto the field with a locker-room speech that told the players it was time to deliver. Because of their bye week and the subsequent forfeit by the Lutheran school, the Cubs felt slightly out of sorts. "It's playoff time. Let's do this!" Coach Adams signed to his team. "They're looking for an upset. We've got to get out there and hit. You've had three weeks of rest. We need one hundred percent from you. Remember, this is a chance of a lifetime."

Jory rose up from the benches in the team's pregame, let's-get-riled-up ritual, jumping rhythmically with his teammates.

His limits were tested early. The coaches had him in the game for the opening kickoff as a blocker. But the ball was kicked short and he scooped it up, ran for two yards, and then dove to the ground as would-be tacklers approached. Then, on the first offensive play of the game, Coach Adams had Jory lined up wide right on a play that would send him sprinting down the sidelines. As he ran, a defender covered him step for step. Trevin lofted a well-thrown bomb that came down just beyond Jory's grasp. He looked for an interference call but didn't get one. No one watching the game from the Wolfpack sidelines would have had any clue that the player who had just run halfway down the field and then missed that catch by inches had pneumonia. It was only on the fourth play, a long run by Trevin for a first down, that Jory was brought to the sidelines.

With their dark gray uniforms, black undershirts, and red numbers, the Wolfpack looked much more formidable than they played. The Cubs dominated with quick passes and Cody Metzner's smashmouth running. They had sloppy moments, but the game was never close. The Cubs gained seventeen first downs in the game and the Wolfpack just five. The final score was 52–6, a humbling defeat for the Wolfpack, whose physical play at times frustrated the Cubs but ultimately failed to deliver points.

Jory was in and out of the game, unusual for a player accustomed to never missing a snap on offense or defense. He missed some long passes that he might normally have come down with. It was the only game that season where he did not score any points for the team. The Cubs had proven something with both Felix and Jory sidelined or marginalized. They could play next-man-up football. The cousins had come through. Gio Visco, the freshman receiver, had ten catches and scored two touchdowns, and Luca Visco intercepted a tipped pass that he ran back for a score.

In the fourth quarter of the game, with the Cubs already sure of their win, Coach Adams had taken out many of the team's starters. Kaden had replaced his brother as quarterback, and Ricardo Terrazas had moved to running back. But the coaches kept their first-string linemen in the game, including Christian Jimenez at right guard. On a routine running play, Christian led the blocking, wrestling his way off the line and creating enough running room for Ricardo, the ballcarrier, to inch ahead. But one of the biggest players on the Wolfpack, a 230-pound lineman, had swung behind the play unblocked and had lunged for a piece of Ricardo's jersey. Dragged forward by Ricardo's determined running, the lineman managed the tackle, but on his way to the turf smashed into the back of Christian's legs.

As the referee whistled the play over, Christian immediately grabbed for his left leg. He writhed and slapped the turf in pain. The referee urgently waved the Cubs' physical trainer onto the field.

Years earlier, Christian had broken his right leg, and the familiarity of the pain made the injury even more sickening to him. He knew it was not a torn muscle or ligament. The bone was broken. He could feel it. An X-ray would later confirm that he had fractured his fibula. Under the gaze of spectators standing on the bleachers, players and coaches lifted Christian up and carried him off the field. It looked like a scene from a battlefield.

Another game, another starter down. With only twenty-three players on the roster, the team's bench was not that deep. In addition to his role as a lineman, Christian was the student body president. He was a natural mentor and leader. Galvin Drake called him the "king of the line" for his leadership abilities. His broken leg was another severe blow to the team, not as dire to their prospects as the loss of Felix. But the offensive line, the unsung heroes of successful high school teams, had been a major difference between the Cubs' performance this year and their dismal final performance the prior year.

The doctor's diagnosis was clear for Christian, as it had been for Felix. He needed at least until December, after the championship game, to recover. "The doctor warned me, 'If you get hit in the same spot, you'll be done for another six to eight months.'" Christian left the CSDR campus that evening stunned and angry. With a huge bag of ice taped to his knee, he gingerly climbed into the front seat of his family's minivan, his high school football career fading in the rearview mirror.

29

The Wicks and the Bombs

Steve Howell, the defensive coordinator for the Leadership Military Academy Wolfpack, was leaving the field, smarting from the crushing of his team's playoff hopes. He made a prediction about the Cubs. They would breeze through the semifinals and advance to the championship, he prophesied, where they would face Faith Baptist for a rematch. The Cubs would lose by two touchdowns, he predicted matter-of-factly. Faith Baptist had the discipline and the athletes to beat the Cubs—again.

Howell, who is from Riverside, said his loss that day was disappointing, but he was happy to see a team from Riverside—the Cubs—advancing deep into the Southern California playoffs.

"I'm proud of them," he said of the Cubs. "I love my city, so it's all good."

The first part of Howell's prediction was widely shared among the Cubs themselves. No one seemed particularly worried by their next opponent, Flintridge Prep, an elite school in the leafy Los Angeles suburb of La Cañada Flintridge, where annual tuition is $41,500 and where 100 percent of graduates head to college. The school boasts such prominent alumni as Mark Geragos, the criminal defense attorney perhaps best known for representing Michael Jackson, among other celebrities.

The Flintridge Wolves had started their season strong, beating Cate and Thacher, two equally elite schools in the Santa Barbara area. Flintridge had notched six wins and suffered two losses so far in the season. Their coaching staff was made up of acclaimed names in the world of California football.

Ramses Barden, the team's offensive coordinator, was both a Flintridge graduate and a former wide receiver for the New York Giants from 2009 to 2012, including their Super Bowl victory against the New England Patriots.

The team's head coach, Russell White, had been first-team all-American at the University of California, Berkeley. During his three-season college career in the early 1990s, he ran for 3,367 yards, an impressive 5 yards per carry, making him the all-time rushing leader for the Golden Bears, a record that still stands. White was selected in the third round of the 1993 draft by the Los Angeles Rams but played only one year and appeared in only five games. (NFL stands for "not for long," White jokes.)

Before the game, White said he was intrigued by the idea of playing a deaf team. It was his first time playing the Cubs, but their deafness didn't come up much in preparations for the game.

"I don't put stress on their being deaf. I put the stress on them being a football team. We treat them as if we are playing Thacher or Cate," he said of the prep schools that were his regular opponents. "Yeah, they communicate different," he said. "But they come in there to knock your block off."

·   ·   ·

So here it was that a scrappy deaf school was up against a prestigious prep school team coached by NFL veterans.

The Cubs players seemed hardly starstruck. On game day, after their dismissal from school, they piled into white vans and headed, as their ritual demanded, to Blaze pizzeria. The fast-food chain treats pizzas the way a delicatessen handles sandwiches: customers line up in front of a glass-encased counter and point to the ingredients they want on their pie. The employees are trained to ask the customers' names, write them down on a slip of paper, and then prepare each pie according to the customers' preferences. But the particular server on duty that day was used to seeing deaf customers, and she improvised, not bothering with names. The players were wearing their red jerseys, so she labeled each pizza with their numbers.

Coming off their 52–6 playoff win against Leadership Military Academy, the Cubs were understandably confident, especially because they had won with Jory still suffering the effects of his walking pneumonia. Giddy and unguarded, teammates signed their predictions to one another as they ate.

"We are going to flatten them and go straight to the championship," said Gio Visco, the freshman receiver who had improved so dramatically during the season, especially on offense, where he sought to fill Felix's shoes. His ten receptions in the game against the Wolfpack were remarkable for a freshman.

"We are a better team than we were last year; every single player is better," Trevin told the players gobbling down their pizzas and drinking water or juice. (No player dared to order a soft drink after the repeated admonishments of their coaches to eat healthily.)

Trevin looked around the restaurant. The coaches were at their own table, far enough away that they wouldn't be able to see what he was signing. "I don't want to say anything too early," Trevin said, pausing. "I don't want to jinx it," he said. "But we should be able to win the championship this year." Trevin's words carried weight, as the captain, as the undisputed star of the team, as a mentor for the younger players.

Hours later, with the game under way against Flintridge, the Cubs had a wrenching feeling that their confidence might have been misplaced.

On what was a chilly night, with temperatures dipping into the fifties, the Cubs scored first, a pass to Jory streaking across the middle—and wide open. Minutes later, Flintridge responded with their own touchdown. The play was an undisguised pass to the flat, and it revealed weakness. The Flintridge receiver took three steps and then cut toward the sidelines. This was not a difficult play to diagnose: the quarterback stared down his receiver, Owen Willingham, a 140-pound freshman, the whole way and then threw it to him. Luca Visco, responsible for covering Willingham, was playing very soft and was backpedaling when the play started. Luca was ten yards away when the ball was thrown. He sprinted to make the tackle, but Willingham had enough time to square up and juke Luca, who could only grab for his waist before being flung to the ground. Ricardo came next, bolting across the field. Willingham was just beyond his fingertips. Another missed tackle. Willingham bolted the forty yards toward the goal line. On the opposite side of the field, Jory saw the catch and with veteran instincts began sprinting, taking an angle that would allow him to catch up with the receiver a dozen yards before the end zone. Jory's mental geometry was perfect: he arrived at the ten-yard line two steps before the Flintridge receiver. But Willingham was nimble enough to run around him. And there was no one else far enough downfield to help make the tackle. Flintridge had answered the Cubs' scoring drive. They kicked an extra point and were within one point of tying the game.

This back-and-forth continued. Soon it was 16–14, a reed-thin lead for a Cubs team accustomed to running over their opponents. "We've got ourselves a football game, gentlemen," said Ramses Barden, the Giants' former wide receiver, to his players.

Although the schools are only about an hour away from each other, the semifinal game was the first time Flintridge had ever played the Cubs. For both teams it was a process of discovery and adjustment. For the Flintridge coaches and players, it was also a novel sensory experience. They had not emphasized deafness to their players before the game, but both coaches found themselves nonetheless intrigued by the overall lack of crowd noise. They were accustomed after a play to hearing some sort of approval—or disapproval—from the stands.

"It was quiet; the crowd was quiet," the head coach, Russell White, said. "I'm used to playing in big arenas, big stadiums. The quiet was kind of weird. But the football was exactly the same."

From the film he had seen, White had expected the main threat to come from Trevin Adams and Cody Metzner, the physical duo of quarterback and running back, both of whom were not afraid to truck a defender standing in their way.

White called the duo "the wick that attaches to the bomb."

"You light that wick and there's an explosion. Those are the ones I've identified who make the magic happen," he said.

That wasn't necessarily wrong. But the coaches realized there was an added component, something that the film they had watched before the game had not fully conveyed. In one of the most incisive comments that opposing coaches had about the Cubs, Ramses Barden described seeing a brotherhood.

"You see it by how they prepare, how they communicate, how they move as one, how they support each other," Barden said. "You can see the family component that bonds them."

Football is about muscle and speed, about athleticism and agility, but then there are what are called the intangibles. The Cubs had epoxy—the common bond of deafness that gave them a sense of mission and unity that allowed many hands to punch as one. Was it enough to get them to the championship? The next two and a half quarters of football would tell.

·   ·   ·

Russell White was correct in his diagnosis: Trevin and Cody were the "the wick that attaches to the bomb." But the bomb on this day had other components. On one drive, Gio caught a well-thrown pass just short of the first-down sticks. Cody got a first down. Jory caught a short pass to the flat for five yards. It was an incremental, grinding drive that ended with Trevin barreling into the end zone and Jory catching a pass for the extra two points.

But Flintridge had their own explosive formula. They caught the Cubs off guard with an unusual-looking play in the second quarter. They lined up in a heavy formation, with a running back stationed in the backfield and a single wide receiver, Noah Willingham, lined up wide right. Ramses Barden, who designed and called the play, described the running back as a way of distracting the defense, as "eye candy." With the heavy formation it clearly looked like a running play. The quarterback faked the pitch to the running back and dropped back. With the exception of Willingham, the entire Flintridge team was blocking for the quarterback. The play resulted in the Cubs having three idle linebackers—the Adams brothers and Ricardo Terrazas. They were immobilized, twitching as they wondered where to commit. After the faked pitch-back, Willingham, the sole receiver, had streaked past the linebackers and had run in between the two Cubs defensive backs, Jory and Luca Visco. The quarterback, Jack Jones, who at six feet, four inches had no trouble seeing over the heads of the oncoming rush, heaved the ball to the end zone, where Willingham leaped to grab the touchdown.

The Cubs headed to their locker room with the thinnest of margins by the standards of eight-man ball, ahead 24–20.

The coaches huddled. Worry filled their faces. Kaveh Angoorani diagnosed what he thought was the main problem. Going into the game, they had seen the main threat from Flintridge as their running game. They had stacked their line against the run, putting Cody Metzner at nose tackle. But Flintridge had thrown over the linebackers with success. "They found our weakness," Kaveh said of Flintridge. The coaches decided to shift the defense, putting three players in the backfield and positioning Gio very deep as safety. This formation would help compensate for the absence of Felix, who had so expertly guarded against the deep threat. They pulled Ricardo and Xavier Gamboa, a hefty lineman, from the lineup, after both had committed sloppy penalties, including a late hit by Ricardo on the quarterback and a block in the back by Xavier.

"Erase the first half from your memories—throw it away," Trevin told his teammates as they sat on the benches in front of their lockers.

The Cubs had the advantage of receiving the ball in the second half, and they didn't waste it. On the third play, Trevin unleashed a bomb to Gio that sailed nearly forty yards. Gio and his defender were step for step, hand fighting all the way down the field. But when the ball arrived, slightly underthrown, Gio located it while the defensive back was still looking downfield. Gio grabbed the ball and then controlled it all the way to the ground. It was a catch you might have expected at the college level, not by a high school freshman. The Cubs continued with a mix of runs and passes that kept the defense guessing; they drove relentlessly down the field. Andrei Voinea's snaps were crisp and automatic. The budding computer programmer's training sessions on the sidelines had paid off. Cody's power running wore down the defense.

And on fourth and goal, the Cubs pulled off a play that crushed the already deflated Flintridge defense. After the ball was snapped, Flintridge blitzed and got the pressure they needed. They were in Trevin's face and milliseconds from a sack that would give them back the ball. Trevin jumped a foot into the air and got a pass off to Jory, who did his own leap to grab it at the goal line. In desperation, the Flintridge defender pulled Jory down by his face mask, sending yellow flags flying. The penalty was inconsequential: Jory was already in the end zone. Watching from the sidelines on the edge of the end zone were two figures hunched over their crutches: Christian and Felix. Both of them looked up to the scoreboard. It was 38–20. The Cubs were managing to win the semifinals without them. The final score—Cubs 58, Flintridge 28—seemed oddly disconnected from the peril that the Cubs had felt at halftime.

As the players gathered to celebrate on the field, the score vanished from the scoreboard, replaced with another set of numbers: 74–22.

At Coach Adams's request, the scorekeepers had put up the humiliating score from the 2021 championship. It would be a week before the Cubs would return to the field in their quest to avenge that scarring loss. Even as they celebrated this semifinal win, Adams wanted the players to reconnect with the agony of last year's final game as they headed into what for many of the players was their last week playing high school football.

30

An Apparition on the Practice Field

The Cubs were in the finals. The game to decide whom they would play in the championship was held the next day in Simi Valley, an hour and a half away. It began with a call to prayer.

Under a bright blue afternoon sky, players from two Christian schools stood on their sidelines, removed their helmets, and bowed their heads. The Faith Baptist Contenders, undefeated and eager to return to the championship for their second year in a row, were on one side of the field. On the other side were the Grace Brethren Lancers, underdogs and smartly dressed in their home uniforms, all black with red lettering and red stripes down the sides of their legs that vaguely evoked the dress pants of the U.S. Marine Corps.

"Please pray with me," said a pastor's voice over the loudspeaker.

"Father God, we are grateful that we can be here on this beautiful day, thankful for everything that you've created. Thankful that we have two schools that recognize that Jesus Christ is the God of the universe and the author and protector of our faith. Lord, I pray that as the young men compete today that they would do so not for the glory of themselves but for the glory of Christ. Lord, I pray that you would watch over the boys today. May they be safe and healthy on the field. May they compete in a way that honors you. Lord, thank you again that we get to be here, and I pray that you receive the glory."

The last time Grace Brethren had won the championship was twenty-two years earlier, and the school was pining for another appearance in the big game. Like so many institutions in California, Grace was relatively young. Founded in 1978, it began as a preschool and then expanded with a donation from unusual circumstances: after a young woman was murdered while jogging in nearby Moorpark, her husband donated the entire proceeds of her insurance policy to fund the expansion of Grace in honor of his wife's love of children. An elementary school, a middle school, and, ultimately in 1989, a high school would take root. The first graduating class had ten students. Total enrollment would eventually swell to around a thousand.

Grace Brethren versus Faith Baptist, the clash of the Christian schools, would prove to be an ominous warning for the Cubs. Faith scored twenty-eight points in the first quarter and then fourteen points in every subsequent quarter. Their victory was merciless. The final score, 70–22, bore a striking similarity to Faith Baptist's win against the Cubs a year earlier, 74–22.

The rematch was set: the Cubs and the Contenders, both undefeated, would meet at a neutral venue, the stadium of Birmingham Community Charter High School in the San Fernando Valley, on Friday, November 18, 2022.

Although a number of important players had graduated from Faith after the championship win, including their quarterback, the team was largely intact. They still had a core of strong, fast, aggressive players and hard-hitting tacklers.

Parker Mills, the running back who had gashed the Cubs' defense a year before, was on fire this season. Now a senior, he had six touchdowns in the Grace game alone. In the quarterfinals a week earlier he had scored five times.

A. C. Swadling, who the previous year had scored two touchdowns and had eighteen tackles against the Cubs, was also having an impressive year. Now the team's starting quarterback, he had twenty-five touchdowns through the air and twelve on the ground and only three interceptions. And he still fulfilled his role on defense as the enforcer, racking up an eye-popping 102 tackles on the season.

Faith Baptist also still had their giant tight end, a player who commanded attention even halfway across the field. Standing six feet, nine inches (he had gained an inch since the previous championship) and weighing 250 pounds, Tracy Bryden towered over his opponents. He would have stood out in an NFL locker room, let alone high school ball in Southern California.

.   .   .

On Saturday evening the Cubs' coaching staff learned they would be facing Faith Baptist again. With the championship only six days away, they got to work. Kaveh Angoorani pored over game film, spending hours analyzing every game Faith had played that season and documenting their play calling in a thick binder. He identified and documented eighty-six separate plays that Faith had run. The team would use this binder as their bible in the week's practices.

The next evening, on Sunday night, the coaches gathered in Keith Adams's office to strategize. One big question was how they would guard against Bryden, the giant tight end. The Cubs were known for their quickness, their agility, and their athleticism, but not their size. They were, on the whole, undersized, especially when compared with Bryden, who stood half a foot above Jory, the Cubs' lanky receiver. Bryden was a full foot taller than the Cubs' defender who would likely be covering him, Gio Visco.

The coaches came up with a plan. They thought to reach out to Damon Biskupiak, a very tall teacher's aide at CSDR. Maybe Biskupiak could come to practice as a stand-in for Bryden?

Michael Mabashov, the assistant coach responsible for the wide receivers and defensive backs, called Biskupiak on FaceTime with the proposal. "We need your help at our practices," Mabashov signed into the phone. "We need someone really tall." Biskupiak, who is six feet, seven inches, agreed to show up at the Cubs' Tuesday practice.

Coach Adams, meanwhile, was busy trying to figure out how he might inspire his players. He printed out a series of pictures that he taped in the hallway of the locker room and the weight room. The photos were of Cubs players crying in anguish after their defeat against Faith Baptist the previous year. There was a shot of Xavier Gamboa staring vacantly ahead with tears rolling down his cheeks; Phillip Castaneda was shown, head bowed, sitting dejectedly on the turf; and there was a close-up of another player covering his eyes in grief. To rub it in, Adams also pasted a close-up shot of the Faith Baptist championship ring.

As far as team psychology went, it was a pretty straightforward approach. Remember the Alamo! But if that didn't drive home the point, Jory Valencia covered every whiteboard he could find in the school's athletic facility with the score of last year's championship loss:

74–22
74–22
74–22

The numbers had become more powerful than any locker-room speech. They were the symbol of disgrace and defeat.

.   .   .

At practice that week, the coaches took to the field carrying the binder that Kaveh had compiled filled with Faith Baptist's plays.

The team met every afternoon, a contrast to the year before, when the final game had been played Thanksgiving week and students had gone home for the holiday, barely preparing for the championship. This year, the championship game was scheduled for the weekend before the Thanksgiving break.

Coach Adams distributed scrimmage pinnies that carried the numbers of the players the Cubs were concerned about. They had jerseys for Parker Mills, the running back; A. C. Swadling, the quarterback; Tracy Bryden, the towering tight end; and Miguel Llerena, a small but shifty running back and receiver.

Biskupiak, the tall teacher's aide, put on the No. 21 jersey. Without pads or a helmet, Biskupiak caught balls and allowed the coaches to demonstrate how they might strip the ball from him. He was good-natured in his role as a real-life tackling dummy. In their binder of plays, the coaches found that Faith liked to throw the ball to their big tight end in the red zone. They practiced disrupting the play.

Coach Adams had another tool in their preparations for the championship. In a measure of how much Faith Baptist was resented in the league for their dominance, coaches from other teams had texted him unsolicited tips and strategies to beat Faith. In his years coaching, Keith Adams said, it was the first time he had received messages like this.

The first message came from Jordan Ollis, the head coach at Chadwick, the team that the Cubs had soundly beaten in the first game of the season. Ollis had put aside any hard feelings from that game and messaged Keith with some well-observed intelligence: The right guard had a tendency to look in the direction where the play is going before the snap. "I'm talking STARES!!!" Coach Ollis wrote. He was "very easy to read," Ollis said.

Keith shared the tip with his players, who were instructed to watch for the tell but not make it too obvious.

Chadwick had also sent Coach Adams film of A. C. Swadling

slamming into the Chadwick running back, Josh Goodman, after the whistle. This type of play was already on Coach Adams's radar. In the championship game the year before, Swadling had been penalized for unsportsmanlike conduct after he punched Jory Valencia in the gut. Keith kept the clip on his phone, and he planned to show it to the refs before the championship. He wanted them to be on alert for it.

Tom Coate, the Grace Brethren coach, also messaged Keith. He offered bullet points of advice. "Stop the run! Make 1 throw the ball," he texted. "Attack them via pass. Their secondary is weak."

Coate seemed particularly upset that Faith had such a huge team. Eight-man ball was usually played by smaller schools that might struggle to put together an eleven-man roster. But Faith had a small army of players. Coate had counted forty-five (the official roster listed thirty-nine). "It is crazy," Coate said. The Cubs, by contrast, had twenty-three players.

The Cubs' coaches and players ran play after play, moving through the possibilities that they had compiled. They classified the plays by probabilities—ranking the ones that Faith ran most often.

·   ·   ·

When the sun set on their Wednesday practice, two days before the big game, the sky west of the CSDR campus lit up with streaks of orange, gray, red, and yellow, the colors seeming to climb the clouds into the darkening blue sky. Mature trees on the horizon stood in silhouette behind this celestial scene. The relentless hum of the on-field generators brought a soundtrack.

A figure emerged on the field with a slight limp, and in the fading light he appeared almost as an apparition. It was Christian Jimenez, the class president, the leader of the Cubs' offensive line, and the player whom a doctor had ordered to stay away from sports, let alone tackle football, for another four weeks at a minimum.

In the days after his injury, Jimenez had posted a message to his friends. He told them that he had reconciled with the notion that he could not return to the field. Yet as the championship approached—the rematch with the team that had left him and his brothers-in-football so physically crushed and emotionally deflated—something snapped inside him.

Christian began to search Amazon for leg braces, and finally he came up with a contraption for $250 that he said would allow him to play in the championship, which also happened to be the final game of his high school career. He tried to make the case to his parents that they had invested so much in him as a football player that to *not* play in the championship game didn't make any sense.

"Well, of course my parents did not support my decision to play," Christian explained. "They were saying, 'Absolutely not. How are you going to play with this injury?' My close friends and everybody around me were saying, 'No, of course don't play.'"

A gifted and persuasive debater, Christian swayed his family. His parents saw him at home working out with his brace, running with it. He managed to convince them and his coaches that he knew his limits and that he would not cross them.

In the back of everyone's mind, including Christian's, was whether he could really make it work. His Amazon-bought brace seemed to support and protect his leg, but not entirely. The brace, he said, only allowed him to run forward and move in certain directions. "I can't run backward," he said. "I will be playing differently for sure. My movements will be more simplified."

So there it was: the ultimate incentive for a lineman to win his battles in the trenches. Being pushed backward was not an option. He could potentially suffer more severe leg damage. He could only move forward.

Christian admitted that the whole time he was trying to persuade everyone he could play, the words of the specialist who had examined his leg echoed in his head.

"The doctor warned me, 'If you get hit in the same spot, you'll be done,'" Christian said. It was not clear what "done" truly meant. A lifetime of pain? A persistent limp? "It was a difficult decision for me," Christian said.

Since his injury, he had spent days on the sidelines, watching on his crutches the practices and the game against Flintridge. Not being in the game ate away at him. It was torture.

"You know, if I'm not on the field and something goes wrong, I can't do anything about it," he said. "This is my last year of high school. I just feel that I can't let this go."

31

Playing with Fire

At 3:15 on a sunny Friday afternoon, a yellow school bus carrying two dozen high school football players made a right turn onto Victory Boulevard in Lake Balboa, California. The Cubs had arrived for their championship game.

Named in honor of soldiers returning from World War I, Victory Boulevard runs along the southern edge of the sprawling campus of Birmingham Community Charter High School, the chosen site for the game. Faith Baptist had played their semifinal as an away game, so they had the right to host the championship. But the office that runs the league had asked if they would be willing to choose a more neutral locale. Faith settled on Birmingham, which had much higher seating capacity than their school's football facilities. And Birmingham was just twenty minutes away from the Faith Baptist campus.

Owing to its proximity to Hollywood, Birmingham High had been the backdrop for a number of television shows, music videos, and commercials over the years. The list of famous alumni from the school was long, including the actors Lisa Bonet, Sally Field, and Terry Gilliam, and the journalist Daniel Pearl.

For the Cubs, driving to Birmingham had been a two-hour slog across the tangled coil of freeways that strangle Greater Los Angeles. The team had left Riverside at noon, sent off by the entire high school student body, who lined the sidewalk leading to the bus. With Felix on crutches at the front of the line, the Cubs walked in pairs, their arms interlocked, a parade of what many considered the finest athletes the school had ever assembled. Christian Jimenez, walking in the middle of the pack, got to the bus and pulled himself into the vehicle using the handrails, a reminder, if anyone needed it, that he was playing with a fractured leg.

Once at Birmingham High, school was still in session when the Cubs walked onto the campus in search of the locker rooms. The curious eyes of Birmingham students scanned these novel visitors. It was not unusual for visiting teams to walk through campus. But as the Cubs' coaches and players signed to one another, Birmingham's students gawked.

In the long shadows of the late afternoon, the Cubs found the stadium, a recently renovated facility that looked nothing like their patchy dirt home field. The players took the measure of the bright green turf, ringed by a newly surfaced track, and the dozens of rows of bleachers that rose to an enclosed press box. It was a stadium fit for a championship game, a facility that would not have looked out of place at a small college.

With hours to kill before their 7:00 p.m. kickoff, the Cubs found a spot near the end zone and stared up at the sky, watching a parade of private jets taking off from the nearby Van Nuys Airport. It was the start of the weekend before Thanksgiving, and scores of wealthy Southern Californians were heading off to Cabo and other warmer places for the holiday.

When the Faith Baptist players arrived at around 4:30, a cinematic standoff ensued. The Faith players walked onto the field and were met with what Parker Mills, the Faith running back, remembered as "death stares."

"Their faces didn't change," Mills said of the Cubs players.

"They were just staring." He took it as a sign that this was a team serious about winning, intent on revenge.

The Faith roster took to the field for their stretches and calisthenics. The loudspeakers blared wordless motivational music. It was the policy of Faith Baptist not to allow songs with explicit or suggestive lyrics. Instrumental music was a safer bet. The cymbals, trumpets, and rousing guitar chords sounded like a cross between a John Williams soundtrack and the *Rocky* theme song.

The Faith players shouted in unison during a round of jumping jacks. "C-O-N-T-E-N-D-E-R-S!" The team's name was a biblical reference, an exhortation to "contend for the faith."

Soon, both teams would retreat to their locker rooms for their final pregame strategizing and pep talks. Faith Baptist and the Cubs had stomped on their opponents all season long. Both were finishing remarkable runs, but one of these teams was about to suffer its first and only loss of the year.

.   .   .

In practices that week, Faith Baptist had discussed their game plan: own the line and no turnovers. Coach Davidson's biggest concern going into the game was how much the Cubs' line had improved since the last championship. If you gave a quarterback like Trevin Adams an extra second or two of protection, the results could be disastrous. He wanted his players to focus on beating the Cubs at the line.

Leading up to the championship, there was strong confidence among players that they would win again. Practice that week had not been ideal—a number of players had been out with colds—but the undefeated season and the memories of crushing the Cubs the previous year had a way of filling them with optimism.

"There was no doubting on the team," said Mills, the running back. "We were going to go up and win." A year earlier, as he was running circles around the Cubs' defense, Mills had told his coaches, "Give me the ball! Give me the ball!" The plan in this game was to do the same.

In the locker room, A. C. Swadling gave what he described as "a quick little prayer before we went out and battled." It went something like this:

Dear Lord, please be with us today as you give us the strength of ten thousand men. Let us tackle, block—and no turnovers. And let us win, please.

In the Cubs' locker room, coaches called for a moment of silence. With the lights turned off, the players sat on benches, hunched over with their elbows on their thighs and their helmets off, heads bowed. Trevin Adams was squeezed next to his brother, Kaden. When the lights came back on, the Adams brothers stood up together as their dad gave the team one last exhortation.

"Let's just play—play with fire," Keith told his team. "Play with all your heart. Play hard, play smart."

Spectators had filed into the stadium in the hundreds, but nowhere near the numbers of the previous year. It was a long trip in dreaded Friday evening Los Angeles traffic. Even some of the Cubs' biggest boosters, including the school's former superintendent, Nancy Hlibok Amann, who had recently taken a more senior job at the California Department of Education, settled for watching the game live-streamed from home. One notable fan in attendance was the deaf actress Marlee Matlin, best known for her performance in *The West Wing*, who, along with Erika Thompson, the head of communications for CSDR, wore a red Cubs sweatshirt and waved cheerleading pom-poms from the stands. Cubs fans in the stadium numbered a little over two hundred, and they bundled themselves against the evening chill. One group of Cubs supporters unfurled a banner that read WE MEET AGAIN. NOW WE STAY UNDEFEATED.

The media, too, were in much more modest numbers than the previous year. There was a film crew gathering clips for the *NFL 360* mini-documentary on Keith Adams, and a reporter and photographer from the Riverside *Press-Enterprise.* The television networks that had swarmed the team a year earlier had stayed away. Were they expecting another rout of the Cubs? Or had they just moved on from the story, distracted by the pandemic and the other disasters, natural and otherwise, that preoccupied California minds? Whatever the reason, the Cubs' coaches and players said they were relieved. The media onslaught, the prying cameras, the daily interviews—they added up to a distraction. Now in this championship they could focus on football.

With the game minutes away, the Faith Baptist marching band played the national anthem and the emcee said a short prayer:

> Our heavenly Father, we thank you so much for these two teams, these coaches, these fans, parents. We thank you for the hard work that's gone into this season. Please bless these players and we pray that you give them safety on and off the field.

As they had the year before, the Cubs won the coin toss and elected to receive the ball. This followed a lucky trend for the Cubs. They had won the right to receive the opening kickoff, which was almost always their preference, in seven out of their eleven games this season, 64 percent of the time. Not only were the Cubs talented, but the oversized coin that refs used to decide who got the ball seemed to like them, too.

The Faith Baptist kicker, a sophomore with a big leg, smacked the ball out of the end zone. The championship game was under way. As was customary in eight-man football with a touchback, the Cubs would start at their own fifteen-yard line.

.   .   .

Coach Davidson was a true believer in the old maxim that stout defenses win the big games in football.

"You can be a prolific scorer all year long, and if a team comes out and really challenges that defensively, it disrupts your game quite a bit," he had said a few days before the championship.

Davidson had taken a business trip to Mexico City in the days leading up to the game, and he had scrolled through film of the Cubs in between meetings and on the plane.

He noted that the Cubs had given up relatively few yards to penalties. "They don't make a lot of mistakes," he said. "They don't give free yardage, like a lot of teams."

He needed to make sure that his players were also as mistake-free as possible. "In a big game, it could be the kiss of death," Davidson said.

With the game under way, all these notions would be tested.

The Cubs lined up in a pass formation with three wide receivers and Cody in the backfield. Trevin called for the snap the way he always did: clapping his hands rhythmically. It was then up to the center, Andrei Voinea, the Romanian American computer programmer, to send him the ball. But on the first clap and with the ball still firmly on the turf under Voinea's fingers, a Faith lineman surged forward, drawing an offside penalty. Was it championship nerves? Or did the Cubs' silent count, unusual for hearing teams, draw Faith offside? Either way, the Cubs were happy to start the game with five free yards.

On the second play of the game, the Cubs kept the same formation, and Jory Valencia streaked downfield, covered step for step by a Faith defensive back who grabbed Jory's left arm as if the two were waltzing. Trevin's pass landed on the artificial turf in front of them, and the back judge launched his yellow flag into the air. Pass interference. Two plays, two penalties for Faith. It was far too early to call these mistakes the "kiss of death," as Coach Davidson had feared, but it was a frustrating start.

On the third play, a Faith player again jumped offside. It seemed that the silent cadence was confounding the Faith Baptist defense. Voinea, the center, took pride in drawing his opponents offside. The quirky snap method was one of the advantages of deafness, he said, and he reveled in exploiting it. "They're used to hearing the quarterback yell and the center snapping the ball instantly," Voinea said. "But I did the opposite. I waited for a few seconds before snapping the ball. It was a big advantage for us."

For Faith's linemen, the snap method was disorienting. For the Cubs, all eyes were on the ball. Crowd noise, trash talk—none of that mattered to them, as Trevin had said. This was "deaf gain" in action.

Three penalties had moved the Cubs all the way to midfield, the easiest big chunk of yards they had gained all season.

Trevin Adams kept the ball on the next play and, led by Cody and Kaden as blockers, got four yards. After three penalty-plagued plays, it felt as though the game of football had finally begun. On the next play, Trevin kept it again and ran all the way to the twenty-two-yard line. The Cubs were already knocking on the door barely one minute into the game.

Faith Baptist sent in their towering tight end, Tracy Bryden, for the next play on defense. Trevin called for the ball from the shot-gun and ran with it again. Instead of running to the opposite side of the field from where Bryden was standing, Trevin ran straight for him. At six feet, one inch, Trevin was eight inches shorter than Bryden. But both Bryden and another lineman missed their tack-les, grabbing and then letting go of Trevin's jersey as he ran for the corner of the end zone. The first touchdown of the game had come relatively easily. With the two-point conversion that followed, the Cubs were up, 8–0.

Faith Baptist's first set of downs would go even faster. After a dozen-yard runback on the kickoff, Faith started their first drive from their own thirty-four-yard line. In eight-man ball this is decent field position, not too far from midfield at the forty-yard line.

Faith lined up in a tight, power running formation, with five players on the line, the quarterback under center, and Parker Mills, the running back, in the backfield. Only one wide receiver was off to the right. The Cubs countered this formation with a very conservative defense: just two players on the line. Behind them were three linebackers and three players deep in the secondary.

David Figueroa, at right guard, was lined up against Tracy Bryden. In the championship game the year before, Figueroa had been intimidated by Bryden's size. But he felt more confident in this game. He knew that Bryden was massive, but not very fast. The play was a pitch-back to Parker Mills, who ran toward the right sidelines. Faith was going with the playbook that had given them so many yards a year earlier.

But as soon as the ball was snapped and pitched back to Mills, Figueroa came off his block and darted across the line. Helped by Luca Visco, who came from his deep safety position, the two Cubs combined for the tackle. Mills had gotten only a couple of yards.

Figueroa, proud that he had slipped past his jumbo opponent, was jubilant. "I wanted to show him, 'Your height means nothing to me,'" Figueroa would say after the game.

On the next snap, Faith tried the same play to the left side, testing the Cubs' run defense. Gio Visco quickly diagnosed the play and made a diving tackle. Mills had gotten another three yards.

On third down, they set up a pass. A. C. Swadling, the Faith quarterback, dropped back. His three receivers ran patterns to the right side of the field, leaving the left side looking as empty as a Monday morning church parking lot. Swadling tucked the ball and used his considerable speed to dash all the way to the goal line. The crowd roared with greater and greater volume the farther he ran.

With Jory Valencia in pursuit, Swadling dove into the end zone at the pylon. As the refs raised their arms to signal the touchdown, the Faith Baptist sidelines set off pyrotechnics that popped and cracked and sent a cloud of smoke wafting across the field.

With just three plays, Faith Baptist had answered the Cubs. After a failed two-point conversion, the Cubs had a slim lead, 8–6.

Faith's powerful kicker sent the ball through the end zone again. The Cubs found themselves once more starting a drive deep in their own territory. A handoff to Cody on the first play got them only two yards. It was time for something bolder.

On the next play, Trevin dropped back to pass and found himself under pressure from a blitz. He threw a long, arcing pass to his first read, Jory Valencia, who was streaking down the right sidelines. It was an audacious throw: the Faith defender had Jory covered so tightly that in the blur of the moment they could have been mistaken as one large body running with four legs. Over their many years playing together, Trevin had built up trust that if he threw the ball in his direction, Jory, the basketball player whose brother was good enough to play in the pro leagues in Europe, would outjump his defender and come down with the ball. "I knew he would catch it," Trevin would later say. The defender, Jackson Simon, who was around the same height as Jory, had other ideas. He had taken the inside position, and with the ball in the air he was now a half step ahead of Jory. It was as if Jackson, not Jory, were the receiver. Jory tried to leap over Jackson to bat the pass away, but his timing was off. Jackson intercepted the ball and, as Jory fell to the turf, stayed on his feet and made a quick U-turn. He ran thirty yards before the Cubs could tackle him. The Faith sidelines set off another round of pyrotechnics, and smoke again hovered over the field like gunpowder mist shrouding a battlefield.

With the interception, Faith Baptist were "feeling it," in the words of Parker Mills. They got down to business with a series of running plays and short passes that brought them to the three-yard line.

A. C. Swadling ran to the sidelines to get the play from Coach Davidson. It was a simple sweep to the left. Swadling kept the ball and ran behind his running back, who tied up the Cubs pursuers just long enough for Swadling to make it to the goal line. Touchdown. An extra-point attempt fell short.

Coach Adams looked up at the scoreboard. With 6:38 left in the first quarter, the Cubs were losing 12–8. A thought crossed his mind. Would this championship game be another disappointment?

32

The Psychology of Winning

As a high school athlete in the 1980s, David Lavallee was voted all-American by coaches in New Hampshire. He was the only soccer player in the state to be given the honor that year. His team was unbeaten and won the state championship. Lavallee was a big part of that, scoring sixteen goals. In an article in the local newspaper, which pronounced Lavallee the high school player of the year, his coach gave a surprisingly frank assessment of his star forward. "He's not the most skilled player in the state, or the team for that matter," the coach was quoted as saying. "It was the rest of his make-up. His character. His willingness not to give up." Lavallee was praised, above all, as a great teammate whose ego never got in the way.

Success in sports almost always involves more than just raw athletic talent. There is the coaching, the practices, the conditioning, the discipline, the luck. But there is also another crucial intangible: the mechanics and the mysteries of successful teamwork. It's what makes team sports, and football in particular, a fascinating study in human behavior.

After high school, Lavallee studied the psychology of sports. What were the social dynamics that made certain teams win and others flop? He devoted his career to the science of sport, drawing on something called social identity theory, which holds that the more that individual team members can relate to the identity of the team, the better the group's performance will be. Research has found that a team can be an extension of a person's sense of self, and when they perceive themselves to share membership in a group, it can become a powerful determinant of the team's overall behavior. "It can give teams an edge," Lavallee said.

For the Cubs, their common bond, their "social identity," was clearly deafness. The team's players and coaches were from a wide variety of ethnic backgrounds—Mexican, Romanian, Ethiopian, Iranian, Ukrainian, Russian, German, and Native American, to name only some of the ancestries. They had varying complexions and came from families with starkly different income levels. Some lived in suburban homes with swimming pools and had mothers and fathers who were teachers with master's degrees. Others had parents who stocked shelves or were farmworkers. What the players had in common was the way they communicated.

The question for the Cubs as they played for the championship ring was whether they had the intangible winning formula and whether "social identity" might help push them over the top.

There was also a bigger question for the team, well beyond the playing field. High school sports are often praised as a way for students to find friendship and support during the rocky periods of adolescence. The Cubs' football program provided something more: As deaf children in a hearing world, Cubs players had experienced bouts of loneliness and disconnect. Intentionally or not, they had been ostracized from the world by hearing people at various points in their lives. Being part of the Cubs gave them a human bond that offered a measure of fortitude and resilience on the field and off.

In 1938, researchers at Harvard University began what has become the world's longest academic study on happiness, one that is still running. The goal was to understand what led to healthy and happy lives. Some of the thousands of people studied in the research went on to successful careers in business, law, and medicine. Others ended up struggling with mental illness and substance abuse. They came from both privileged backgrounds and Boston's inner city.

But the most significant contributor to happiness, the study found again and again over the decades, was not money or fame, but relationships with other people. Close relationships helped delay mental and physical decline.

"Loneliness kills," said Robert Waldinger, director of the study, in a TED talk. "It's as powerful as smoking or alcoholism."

The Cubs had made it to the championship. Win or lose, they had already forged enduring friendships and memories. Win or lose, they had a brotherhood that would be with them for a lifetime.

33

The Throw

As the night settled in, the temperature had dropped to fifty degrees on the field. But the game, now halfway through the first quarter, was heating up. Coach Davidson removed his blue Faith Baptist varsity jacket.

On their third drive of the game, the Cubs used one of their favorite plays, one that they had successfully run throughout the season but that had failed a number of times against Faith Baptist a year earlier. It was a simple screen pass that required timing and patience. This time, they displayed both. The Cubs' linemen let the Faith defenders rush past them as Trevin dropped back with the ball. With the defensive line bearing down on him unblocked, Trevin rolled out right and threw a perfect pass to Cody, who was crossing ten yards ahead of him. Just as the play was designed, Cody had a vast expanse of green turf in front of him. He ran up the right sidelines thirty yards before being pushed out of bounds. It would have been a triumph and a much-needed morale booster had it not been for a yellow flag shooting into the air. Jory was called for holding. The huge gain was erased, and the Cubs made the demoralizing walk back to their own twenty-yard line. It was a deflating start to what the Cubs hoped would be their comeback.

In an attempt to make up for the penalty yards, the Cubs called an ambitious play. Gio Visco dashed downfield, losing his defender. He was wide open and poised for an easy touchdown. But Trevin heaved the ball well beyond Gio's reach. The pass was uncatchable. As it sailed, Gio raised one hand and seemed to curse it, as if the inflated piece of pigskin had personally offended him. It was one of Trevin's worst throws of the season, and it came just as the Cubs needed some momentum. Trevin gripped his own face mask in frustration. The interception, the holding penalty, the horrible pass. This is the time to refocus, he thought to himself.

To settle down the offense, the Cubs fed Cody the ball, play after play. He smashed into the Faith Baptist line, a game of ground and pound that moved the ball progressively down the field. When they had reached the twenty-eight-yard line, Cody was slow to get up. The hard hits were already taking their toll. It was fourth down and four yards to go.

Coach Adams signed the next play: They were going for it. Another run. The Cubs desperately needed this play to keep the drive alive and to turn this losing game around. The call was for Trevin to keep the ball and run left. But the play looked doomed from the start. Two Faith defenders had successfully read the run, and they were converging on Trevin, who had nowhere to go but backward. As any football fan knows, a successful quarterback needs more than just a strong arm and nimble feet. The great quarterbacks have an ability to process information at lightning speed. As he backpedaled, Trevin recognized that one of the defensive players bearing down on him was the defensive back who had been covering Gio Visco but had abandoned his assignment to join the blitz. This was a crucial observation. Five yards behind the line of scrimmage, Trevin was milliseconds from being slammed to the ground. One of the Faith defenders had wrapped him up with a bear hug from hell. With his body at a forty-five-degree angle on the way to the ground, Trevin somehow managed to heave the ball downfield. It was the mother of all Hail Marys. But it went far enough that Gio, now wide open on the ten-yard line, ran back to catch this desperate throw. He got under the ball, caught it, and scrambled to turn back toward the goal line. He made it to the two-yard line before being tackled. First and goal. Trevin's throw was not so much improvisation as a magic trick, a broken play fixed by football fairy dust and computer-chip-fast mental calculations. On the next snap, Cody took a handoff and dove into the azure-colored end zone.

After a failed two-point conversion, the Cubs were now back in the lead, 14–12, with one minute left in the first quarter.

34

Blocking and Tackling

It was time for the Cubs' defense to stiffen. As Faith tried to move down the field, Trevin came up to make a bruising tackle. And Kaden nearly intercepted a pass that had been thrown in a panic as Cubs linemen put intense pressure on the quarterback.

Faith eked out a first down. But at their own thirty-four-yard line, the Cubs made an important statement.

Faith lined up in a running formation, with Parker Mills in the backfield. The play was a quick handoff to Mills, who began to follow his line of blockers to the left. Trevin Adams, with no receivers downfield to worry about, shot through the line from his middle-linebacker position. He grabbed Mills around the chest and began to push him back, joined by his brother, who made sure Mills ended on the ground. The Adams brothers had demolished a play that a year earlier had given the Cubs so much agony. The Cubs' message to Faith Baptist was that Parker Mills, the running back who had averaged four touchdowns a game this season, would not be a factor in the championships. Mills had described the season until the championship game as his best "by ten miles." The Cubs wanted this to be the end of the road.

After another ball was nearly intercepted and a well-defended pass was dropped, Faith Baptist was forced to punt for the first time in the game.

The Cubs capitalized on Faith's failed drive. They ran another screen pass, nearly identical to the one that had been called back for holding. As the Faith defenders rushed in, Trevin lofted the ball to Jory, who caught it and ran for nine yards, to the Faith Baptist thirty-six-yard line. Coach Davidson looked at his linemen and shrugged. How could you miss that?

The Cubs would make another statement, this time right in front of Davidson's nose. On a first down at the Faith Baptist twenty-two-yard line, Gio Visco was lined up wide left. He caught a screen pass and headed upfield. Blocking for him was Cody, who cleared the way by pancaking a Faith defender in plain view of the Faith sidelines. It was only the second quarter, but the Cubs had already shown they were a different team in one very important respect: they were manhandling Faith Baptist defenders.

Wizened football coaches will often recite the maxim that blocking and tackling are what win games. The Cubs were sending their opponents flying and bringing them to the turf.

Trevin would slam his way across the goal line at the end of the drive, and the Cubs found themselves up 22–12.

.   .   .

A. C. Swadling, who had woken up that morning with a fever, added to his discomfort by dislocating his thumb as he tried to stiff-arm a Cubs defender. He went to the sidelines, where a trainer snapped it back into place and wrapped protective tape around it.

With the quarterback sidelined, Faith ran five straight running plays into the teeth of the Cubs' defense. They managed one first down, but on fourth and nine they tried a screen pass that was dropped.

The Cubs got the ball back on their own twenty-yard line.

Ahead by ten points, the Cubs might have been tempted to conserve their lead by keeping the ball on the ground. But Coach Adams called a series of aggressive passes instead. It was more risky, but it quickly brought them down the field again. A perfectly thrown ball to Gio got them to midfield. And in a sign of their fearlessness, the Cubs ran the same play that earlier in the game had resulted in an interception. Jory was lined up with the same defender, Jackson Simon. What would follow was more basketball than football.

Trevin dropped back as Tracy Bryden, the giant defensive end, came around the edge, his arms eight feet in the air, ready to block the pass. Trevin had just enough time to heave a bomb toward Jory, who this time was beating his defender. Slightly underthrown, the pass forced Jory to slow down, and he and Jackson Simon jumped into the air simultaneously to grab it. Four hands were in the air, reaching for the heavens. The ball hit Jory on the face mask, but as it bounced away, Jory caught it on the rebound. It was another magic trick, another high-stakes, risky play. And another touchdown. The Cubs were up by sixteen.

The game was accelerating now. With their running game going nowhere and passes off-line, Faith Baptist went three and out and punted for the second time.

·　　·　　·

With his broken leg, Christian Jimenez had not been sure how much of the championship game he could bear to play. Wrestling in the trenches with a fractured fibula against an aggressive and physical team is not for the fainthearted. The Cubs had not of course advertised the fact that one of their linemen was playing with a broken leg, but it was evident from the brace that he was recovering from some kind of injury. In the first quarter, after a play where he had helped open a hole for Trevin to run through, he found himself on the ground with the Faith defender he had just blocked. He felt a very sharp pinch in his fractured leg, and doubts filled his mind.

"At that moment, I thought I didn't want to play anymore," Christian said. "I didn't want to get hurt any worse. I knew this was the championship game and I had to give it my all. But I had that fear. I thought I might not be able to get up. I thought I might have fractured it again."

Christian made it to his feet with the help of the Faith player he had just blocked, an act of kindness by his rival. He got up off the turf like an old man standing up from a rocking chair, gingerly keeping his leg straight as it continued to throb with pain.

But he mustered the courage to stay in the game, and on the very next snap he was blocking Tracy Bryden, the giant defensive end.

At the end of the second quarter, with the Cubs leading by sixteen points and again on the move, Christian adjusted his usual footwork. He avoided putting weight on his back leg, his broken leg.

On a third down and three, the call was for Trevin to keep the ball and run for the first down behind Christian. When the ball was snapped, Christian gripped his defender and somehow got him to the turf. A few feet away, Cody pancaked the tight end. Trevin found his way through the splayed bodies to the ten-yard line, more than enough for the first down. The aftermath of the play looked like a Civil War reenactment, with blue uniforms prone on the field of battle. The Cubs were winning the war of the trenches. And they were led by a lineman with a broken leg.

On the next play, again running behind his blockers, Trevin scored. Cubs 36, Faith Baptist 12.

.   .   .

With just a minute left before the half, Faith Baptist was desperate. They needed points to give them some hope during the halftime break. From their own thirty-one-yard line, they tried a screen pass to Parker Mills. The only problem was that Trevin Adams knew this play very well; he had been running it against Faith Baptist all game long with success. From his middle-linebacker position, Trevin read the eyes of the quarterback, jumped in front of Parker Mills, and intercepted the ball, running thirty-three yards for the touchdown. A. C. Swadling, who had thrown the pass, bolted to catch up with Adams and dove at his feet. Swadling missed and forlornly slid on his back toward the sidelines, his eyes cast up to the stadium lights and dark night sky.

California School for the Deaf, Riverside 42, Faith Baptist 12.

The teams left the field for halftime.

Was this game over?

35

College Dreams

In the late 1980s, Roger Adams approached the football coach at Lincoln High School in Stockton with a proposal.

Adams had a deaf son, a junior, who was enrolled at the California School for the Deaf in Fremont, California. But his son loved football, and Lincoln, the biggest high school in Stockton, had a powerhouse football program. Could they take this boy as a student and let him play on the football team?

Keith Adams's father had put forward this unusual arrangement. The idea was that Keith would attend Lincoln during the football months and then return to the deaf school in the off-season. The proposal was also uncharted territory for Jim Rubiales, the Lincoln football coach. He had no previous experience with deafness.

"We talked about the obstacles that he might encounter," Rubiales remembered decades later. "He couldn't hear and he couldn't speak. I went to our principal and asked what could we do for him. They were extremely accommodating. They said, 'We will get him a translator.'"

The football program at Lincoln High School was a crucial part of the Stockton community in the 1980s. The school's stadium had a capacity of six thousand people, and on game days very often it was full. Hundreds more spectators pressed their noses to the chain-link fence at the edge of the end zone to watch the games from the parking lot. The bleachers came to within a dozen yards of the sidelines, so the stadium was considered one of the best places to watch a high school game anywhere in California. And the games were often dazzling: The football program produced athletes who left for careers in college and the NFL. Shante Carver, a Lincoln alum, was selected in the first round by the Dallas Cowboys in the 1994 draft. Brandin Cooks, another Lincoln alum, was also chosen in the first round of the NFL draft a decade later and had a standout career as a wide receiver for a number of NFL teams.

This was high school football of the highest level, and Rubiales remembers having his doubts about whether Keith Adams, the deaf student, would fit in.

"At first, I was like, is this going to work? Everything tells you this *isn't* going to work." Even with an interpreter, Rubiales anticipated times when he might have trouble communicating with Adams. In the heat of a close game, in the seconds before the ball was snapped.

All those fears were allayed when Keith Adams took to the field. Rubiales put him at defensive end, where Keith would play with ferocity. "He was very physical, very quick; he played with emotion and never quit," Rubiales said. "Never."

Tim Tuitavuki, a teammate on defense with Adams, remembers Keith as one of the most physically gifted players on the team.

"He was just a monster," said Tuitavuki, now an attorney in Stockton. "Superstrong, superfast. Full speed was his only speed. Being deaf, he had a heightened sense of his vision," Tuitavuki said. "He was the fastest off the ball out of us defensive linemen."

In the three decades after Keith Adams played defensive end for

Lincoln, Coach Rubiales would lecture the subsequent generations of players on the importance of avoiding offside penalties.

"I had a guy who never once jumped offside," Rubiales would tell his students. "How did he do that? He's deaf. A defensive player shouldn't be listening to anything. You watch the ball. That's what Keith did. It was all by sight."

Tuitavuki, Adams's teammate, remembers it being slightly more nuanced than that. The referees *had* called Adams offside a few times. But they had been wrong.

"When we went back and looked at the film, he was just so quick it *looked like* he was offside," Tuitavuki said. "But he wasn't."

Adams became what his coach described as a celebrity on campus. Spectators at Lincoln games would watch him sack the quarterback and tackle runners for a loss; then there would be chatter in the grandstands.

"There was a buzz in the stadium," Rubiales said. "Kids would turn to their parents and friends. Do you know that guy can't even hear? He can't talk or hear. Watch him when he goes to the sidelines. He's signing with that other guy." The other guy was Kirk, Keith's older brother, a Lincoln alumnus, who was hired by the school to be Keith's interpreter.

Keith had one very important spectator in the stadium to think about. Carol Bella had little trouble persuading her father, a big football fan, to drive to Stockton to watch Keith play. His high school sweetheart was in the bleachers. It was the stuff of afternoon television specials.

As a deaf player on an all-hearing team, Keith was held back in one respect, his brother said. Keith was put at defensive end because he could look in at the play and did not need to communicate with his teammates. But Kirk believed Keith would have excelled in the middle of the field, where he could have had an even greater influence on the success of his defense.

"The position he should have been playing was middle linebacker," Kirk said. "But because it was a hearing team, everything was verbal. Really, he couldn't play that position because of the communication.

"On an all-deaf team it would be no handicap; it's no big deal. They would play based on hand signs, so if someone needs to make an audible, it's not a problem, everybody is looking at him. But on a hearing team, you just can't do that."

As happened often at the school, recruiters from the nation's top colleges scouted Lincoln for talent. They wanted to know more about that defensive end, Keith Adams.

"Everybody came around and they watched film and they said, he's a Division I football player," Coach Rubiales said.

But when they found out Keith was deaf, the conversation changed. Let me check with my head office about this, Rubiales remembered the recruiters saying. We'll think about it, others would say. School after school came back with the same answer: we can't accommodate a deaf student in our football program.

Keith Adams was voted lineman of the year in the San Joaquin Athletic Association. Yet all but a few colleges declined to take him.

"It was too easy to move on to the next guy," Tuitavuki, his teammate, said. Keith, a prodigious talent on the field, had hit a wall. Not because of his football abilities, but because he was a deaf kid in a hearing world.

Adams ended up playing football at California Polytechnic State University at San Luis Obispo. The school agreed to provide an interpreter for him and gave him a football scholarship. His brother, Kirk, meanwhile, became a search-and-rescue helicopter pilot in the U.S. Air Force and did ten combat tours in Afghanistan and Iraq. "We praised the Lord he came back safe," Linda Adams said of her son Kirk.

Keith was defensive end at San Luis Obispo but became frustrated. The interpreter whom the school provided was lousy, and he found himself lonely.

Jim Rubiales remembers receiving a call. The telephone operator informed him that someone named Keith Adams was calling from San Luis Obispo. This was the era before smartphones, and the operator told Rubiales that Adams would type messages and she would relay them, the system known as TTY. The conversation went on for a while.

"He was almost apologizing to me," Rubiales remembered. "He said, 'Coach, I'm just really unhappy. I can't communicate. There's a translator here, sometimes he comes, sometimes he doesn't. I have no friends; no one talks to me. I just can't do this anymore.'"

Rubiales realized that Adams was telling him he needed to leave the San Luis Obispo program.

"I could feel him crying. And it made me cry," Rubiales said. "I told him, 'You have to do what you got to do.' You have to be happy. He was apologizing to me for letting me down. I said, 'You're not letting me down.'"

Adams transferred to Gallaudet, the deaf university in Washington, D.C. The home of the huddle. He played for the Gallaudet Bison for two years as middle linebacker, the position he had always wanted to play in high school. The Bison were a Division III team, and they did terribly in the years that Keith played there. They won only a handful of games.

But that wasn't the point of going to Gallaudet. Keith would find the camaraderie and friendship that had eluded him at San Luis Obispo. He enjoyed his time on the team. Most important, he was reunited with Carol Bella. When the two married, the wedding was designed to be deaf-friendly: The guests were arrayed at tables where everyone had a line of sight to the emcee. The ceremony was in sign language, but there was interpreting for the hearing guests.

Two decades later, Keith Adams found himself coaching his own two sons in a league title game. It was the star-studded, all-deaf high school squad that he dreamed of, but never had. The rejections from colleges, the loneliness at San Luis Obispo—all of that was in the rearview mirror. His boys had also once played on hearing teams, local youth football programs where they would also experience a degree of alienation. Now they were members of the Cubs brotherhood. And Keith Adams just needed to prove that an all-deaf team could win, for the first time in their history, the championship in a league where most of their opponents were hearing teams. Winning would be a validation. More important, as his defensive coordinator once said, winning would be forever.

36

"That Kid Can Play Anywhere"

The fans at the championship game were segregated across the field from one another. Faith Baptist supporters sat on the side of the field that had the indoor press booth at the top of the bleachers. Cubs fans were seated on the opposite side of the field. But there was a lone spectator far from the cheering sections. Jim Perry, the president of the Southern Section of the California Interscholastic Federation, the governing body for all high school athletics in the state of California, sat in a folding chair just beyond the end zone and beneath the scoreboard. From a game-watching perspective, it wasn't the best seat in the house. But by sitting on his own at the far end of the field, he avoided the perception that he was with one team or the other. Perry, a former basketball player at the University of Southern California, was not *entirely* alone. He had with him a very important piece of hardware, a dark wood plaque with the words CHAMPIONS 2022 inscribed over the top. Bundled against the evening chill in his chair, Perry was ready to present it to the winner.

.   .   .

When the teams came back onto the field for the second half, Faith Baptist was primed for a rebound. In the locker room at halftime, Faith coaches had told their players to believe in their abilities. This is nothing, they said. We've done this before. We are down by four touchdowns, but we've scored that many in a half before. Let's do it again. Parker Mills thought it was a good pep talk, and he convinced himself they could pull it off. Sometimes the second half of a football game looks and feels nothing like the first. Faith Baptist would need to start off with a bang. They lined up to receive the kickoff.

The Cubs had a habit of trying onside kicks even when they didn't need to, even when they were well ahead. The philosophy was that even if it worked only 20 percent of the time, the coaches had enough faith in their defense that they didn't mind taking the risk. The coaches had sent out Jory Valencia to kick, and as he ran toward the ball, he did little to disguise his intentions. He turned his body sideways and used the inside of his foot to slap the ball, as if he were passing a soccer ball to a nearby teammate. The ball zipped off the tee, skidding past one Faith Baptist player and hopping beyond the reach of another. Darius Zarembka, a skinny sophomore wide receiver for the Cubs, sprinted toward the ball. It had already gone the requisite ten yards to be up for grabs. Zarembka dove and then slid down the right sideline, snatching the ball before it went out of bounds. The fumble drills, the ones where coaches had urged players to "eat grass," had paid off. The entire Cubs' sideline leaped into the air in celebration. It was their first successful onside kick in the game, and it came as they were already leading by thirty points.

On the Faith sidelines, players smacked the top of their helmets in disbelief. The hope that the halftime speeches had given them evaporated. Parker Mills thought to himself, Damn, we are going to lose.

Watching from the bleachers was Coach Jordan Ollis of Chadwick. Chadwick had played both Faith and the Cubs during the regular season and lost to both. But Ollis marveled at the audacity and determination of the Cubs.

He thought to himself that he had never seen a team play so hard. On every play. Even with the team up by four touchdowns, he saw Trevin scolding his brother at the smallest imperfections. The intensity of this team, Ollis thought. That's why they were so fun to watch. He was especially impressed that the Cubs were dominating without their most versatile and athletic player, Felix Gonzales. In Chadwick's 54–16 loss to the Cubs, Felix had been their leading scorer, with three touchdowns. Felix had also been the team's leading tackler. Now, in the championship, with Felix on the sidelines leaning on his crutches, the Cubs were still winning big.

Coach Davidson, his jacket back on, watched with his hands in his pockets as the Cubs' offense marched down the field again. This was a different team from the one they had played the year before. Faith had been out-blocked and out-hit in this game, he thought. The Cubs were displaying a mastery of the fundamentals so crucial to winning. The physicality of the team deeply impressed him. His players were getting knocked around so much it almost looked as if they were on roller skates. The Cubs, he realized, had spent months in the weight room. And they were playing complementary football, a blend of passes and runs, that was hard to defend against.

On first down at the eleven-yard line, Trevin kept the ball and dashed toward the left pylon of the end zone. He was met by Parker Mills, the two-hundred-pound running back. Trevin lowered his shoulder and bumped his way for a touchdown. The referee raised his hands to signal a touchdown, and Trevin casually handed the ball to the ref.

With the exception of special teams, Trevin Adams had nearly done it all. He had thrown touchdowns and run the ball into the end zone. He had intercepted passes and tackled Faith running backs for a loss. By the end of the night, he would be given credit for a remarkable sixty points. This was the iron-man football that eight-man coaches spoke about, playing both sides of the ball, a marathon of running, blocking, and tackling, a two-and-a-half-hour, nearly continuous wrestling match.

After the next kickoff to Faith, all eyes would turn to Trevin again. A sack by Dominic Turner and David Figueroa had pushed Faith Baptist back ten yards. The Faith quarterback, A. C. Swadling, was on the sidelines again getting his thumb treated, and on third down Christian Kim, the backup quarterback, took a snap. He threw a dart intended for Parker Mills, but Trevin Adams jumped in and snagged the ball as if he were having a catch with friends in the park. Adams ran it back, shrugged off an attempted tackle by the quarterback who had just thrown the interception, and scored another touchdown.

Just as his father had made spectators sit up in their seats and watch at Lincoln High School, Trevin Adams had scored so many points and made so many plays that all the Faith Baptist coaches could do was to shake their heads. "No. 4, what a player," Coach Davidson would say after the game. "He can throw and he can run. That kid can play anywhere."

Faith Baptist managed two touchdowns in the third quarter, a desperate attempt to make the score more respectable. They showed flashes of the great team they had been all season, including an effortless pass from Swadling to Mills in the end zone. But the Cubs' scoring machine did not let up. By the end of the third quarter the score was Cubs 64, Faith Baptist 26.

Before the fourth quarter began, the officials and coaches conferred for a drawn-out discussion over whether to run the clock, as the regulations called for in lopsided games. Faith Baptist resisted. "It's a championship game. Let them play," Coach Davidson said of his players. "They are losing, but that's okay. It's good for them to learn how to win and to learn how to lose. And do both with grace. I didn't win everything in life. And a lot of time I think losing teaches you more than winning."

Davidson didn't think they had a chance to prevail in the game, but he wanted to compete to the fullest.

"I know some people think it's demoralizing," he said. "To me it builds character."

The referees overruled Davidson and said regulations called for the clock to run without interruption when a team is losing by more than thirty-five points at the start of the fourth quarter, as was the case in this game.

The fourth quarter commenced, and even with the accelerated clock the Cubs scored twice more.

With forty-two seconds left in the game, the Cubs kicked off one final time to Faith Baptist. Out of habit, the Faith marching band played a drumroll as Richard Rios kicked off. Parker Mills, deep to receive, scooped up the ball and jogged it up the sidelines. He was lightly shoved out of bounds by Jory Valencia.

With twenty-two seconds left, Faith Baptist ran one more perfunctory play, a deep pass that was nearly intercepted. Cubs fans and players stormed the field and yelped for joy.

The scoreboard, a large black and purple screen framed by the night sky, displayed the championship score. CUBS 80, FAITH BAPTIST 26.

37

"You Guys Deserved This"

In the euphoria of victory, it was hard to process the scene that came immediately after the final whistle. As the players from both teams lined up in single file and walked toward one another for the traditional handshake, A. C. Swadling pointed to each Cub player as they passed. "You can hear me?" Swadling asked. "You can hear me, right?" He repeated the question again and again as he walked across the field. When the greeting line was completed, Swadling told his teammates that they had been misled: the Cubs players could actually hear. It was an odd, and insulting, way to end the night. Asked about it later, Swadling would say that during the game he had called out to Gio Visco, "Hey, No. 2!" and Visco had waved at him. "I was really confused," Swadling said.

But there was nothing to be confused about. Gio Visco is profoundly deaf and has been from birth. It was as if Swadling didn't believe that a deaf team could have beaten Faith Baptist, the powerhouse of eight-man football in Southern California. Even in victory, the Cubs were on the receiving end of mockery, although unaware of it at the time.

On the Cubs' side of the field, there was rapture and jubilation. After walking through the greeting line, the team had gathered around Jim Perry, the California Interscholastic Federation official. A sea of CSDR fans had mobbed the field, standing packed around the team.

Perry held up the championship plaque with his right hand.

"Gentlemen," he said. "Congratulations!"

The Cubs cheered, but with a delay. They looked to Julie Hurdiss, a CSDR interpreter, for translation.

"There are 650-some schools that wish they were playing tonight," Perry said. "You are the last ones standing." It was actually 560 schools in Southern California that would have loved to be playing in a championship that night, 48 of which play eight-man ball. But in the emotions of the moment, Perry could be forgiven for the slight inaccuracy.

Perry handed the trophy to a beaming Coach Adams, who grabbed it with two hands and hoisted it above his head to the cheers of the fans.

Perry watched as the Cubs celebrated, his bright white hair testament to the decades he had spent in high school sports. His eyes filled with tears. "It's why kids play," he said, pausing to gather himself. "All they want is a chance," he said. "It's a great night."

Standing apart from the throng of celebrating players was Felix Gonzales, alone on his crutches. It was too uncomfortable to be in there with so many people crowding around, he explained. He reflected on the score of the game, 80–26, and how it had been flipped around from their 74–22 defeat the previous year. The game had been difficult to watch at times for him, especially when he saw mistakes. He wished he had been playing. It gnawed at him. But the victory still inspired him. "They did their job," he said of the team. "And they did it very well."

Caught up in celebration, the Cubs were not in a frame of mind to analyze what had happened in the second quarter that had allowed them to turn things around. Even in the weeks after the game, no one could quite explain it. It was as if they had reached deep inside themselves and found a wellspring of willpower and drive, an intangible force that exists within all of us. Yes, they had put in the hours in the weight room, but so had their opponents. Yes, they had practiced their plays over and over again. But so had Faith Baptist. They had cast aside the doubt that had haunted them after the previous year's championship. They had united around what society told them was a deficit and made it a gain.

Jordan Ollis, the Chadwick coach, stood on the field amid the revelry and marveled at the notion that the Cubs had pulled off this victory without Felix, without their star athlete. Ollis approached Coach Adams and through an interpreter offered his congratulations.

"Y'all were on a different level from every team in the state," Ollis said. "There's no doubt who the best team is—it's not even close. Not even close," he repeated for emphasis. "Y'all were *so* good this year. And how hard you played! Congrats, man. You guys deserved this."

Coach Adams stood on the field in a baseball cap and a black Cubs zip-up hoodie. He took a moment to reflect on the championship victory. He was reminded of his years playing at Lincoln High, and the colleges that had turned away when they found out he was deaf. Now he was showing the world what a squad of deaf coaches and deaf players could do. They had leveraged deafness. They had come through the window, not the door.

"We showed them that deaf people can do anything," Adams said.

He scanned the field. His wife, Carol, and sons, Trevin and Kaden, stood with his mother, Linda, whom decades earlier Keith had asked what sunshine sounds like. Christian Jimenez, in his leg brace, walked gingerly across the field. Phillip Castaneda, the one-time homeless running back who had run out of eligibility this season, had come down from the bleachers to congratulate his former teammates.

And Kaveh Angoorani, his coaching partner whose unlikely journey had brought him from the streets of Tehran to the subdivisions of Riverside, was already talking about the Harley he was going to buy and the rides he would take past the Joshua trees in the high desert of California.

Keith spoke about the two seasons, the big loss, and then the big win. It felt like a film, he said. "It's a good ending. We beat them with a perfect record. And we're closing out the movie."

"Let the credits roll."

Acknowledgments

By its very title, this is a book about boys and men and their quest for football glory. I thank the players and coaches for allowing me to be a constant set of prying eyes on the sidelines, in team meetings, at meals, and in their living rooms. But in thinking about the long list of people who supported me and were so enthusiastic in seeing that this book get written, I find myself, as with so many things in life, mentally scrolling down a long list of women, in this case mainly deaf women, who helped behind the scenes.

Reporting this book meant moving to Riverside on a tight budget and traveling back and forth to my home in Northern California. And one person more than anyone else made this possible: Teresa Maxwell, a senior administrator at CSDR, offered me her spare bedroom in Riverside. As a hearing person in a deaf household, it was up to me to adjust. But Teresa went out of her way to accommodate me, fretting about squawking smoke alarms and any other sounds that might inconvenience her guest but wouldn't bother her in the least. At CSDR, the former superintendent Nancy Hlibok Amann and the head of the athletics program, Laura Edwards, both went well beyond the call of duty to assist me in navigating the school and community. Erika Thompson, the head of communications for the school, put up with my incessant questions. Crucially, this book would not have been possible without my excellent ASL interpreter, Melika Angoorani, who has such a bright future in front of her, whether it be in the world of interpreting or whatever other field she chooses. Thanks also to the other interpreters who tirelessly translated long interviews: Sabrina Torres, Mara Foley Bowdidge, Julie Hurdiss, and Caleb Thompson.

But I'm jumping the gun. This book never would have gotten off the ground without the support of my wife, my constant sounding board and editor, who encouraged me so enthusiastically despite the extra chores that my long absences would produce. The book also never would have happened had my editor at *The New York Times*, Julie Bloom, not backed the idea of dashing to Riverside to write the story that inspired it. Thanks, as well, to all my colleagues at the *Times* who put up with my absence and covered for me. By the same token, there would have been no book had my agent, Jane Dystel, not suggested I write it! And I was the world's luckiest first-time author to have landed on such a gentle, empathetic editor and master of detail as Jason Kaufman, the executive editor at Knopf Doubleday who believed in the story from the start and combed through the manuscript with both meticulousness and vision.

I thank the experts at Gallaudet University and all the professors and scientists who generously gave their time to help me understand Deaf Culture, education, and society. Un grand merci à Anne Picaud de l'Institut National de Jeunes Sourds de Paris pour m'avoir accueilli à l'institut.

Thanks to the professional photographer Eric Melzer for taking excellent pictures, of course, but also being brave enough to be the manuscript's first reader. And my gratitude goes to Beth Duff-Brown and my brother, Pierre Fuller, who has two books already under his belt, for reading snippets along the way. And to my parents, David and

Isabelle, who listened for hours over the phone as I recounted every last detail of my reporting from Riverside.

I've left out many people at CSDR and in the deaf community in general. Suffice it to say that I was constantly surprised by your hospitality, your patience, and your generosity.

Illustration Credits

ABOUT THE AUTHOR

THOMAS FULLER is a correspondent for *The New York Times* based in Northern California. He has reported from more than forty countries for the *Times* and the *International Herald Tribune*. He spent his early years in Tuckahoe, New York, and lives with his wife, also a journalist, and two children in the East Bay of San Francisco. He is a long-suffering fan of the New York Jets.